John

Happy Birthday

Love

Boo, Douglas & Laura

x x x x x x

AINSLEY HARRIOTT'S
GOURMET EXPRESS 2

AINSLEY HARRIOTT'S
GOURMET EXPRESS 2

WINDING
STAIR
PRESS

Ainsley Harriott's Gourmet Express 2
Original edition © 2001 by Ainsley Harriott
North American edition © 2002 by Winding Stair Press
The moral right of the author has been asserted.
First Published in Great Britain by BBC Worldwide Ltd, 80 Wood Lane, London W12 0TT

National Library of Canada Cataloguing in Publication Data

Harriott, Ainsley
  Ainsley Harriott's Gourmet express 2

Includes index.
ISBN 1-55366-256-3

1. Quick and easy cookery. I. Title. II. Title: Gourmet express 2.

TX833.5.H372 2002   641.5'55   C2001-903978-6

Winding Stair Press
An imprint of Stewart House Publishing Inc.
290 North Queen Street, #210
Etobicoke, Ontario, M9C 5K4
Canada
1-866-574-6873
www.stewarthouse.com

Executive Vice President and Publisher: Ken Proctor
Director of Publishing and Product Acquisition: Joe March
Production Manager: Ruth Bradley-St-Cyr
North Americanization: Alison Maclean and Laura Brady

Recipes developed and written in association with Silvana Franco
Studio photographs by Gus Filgate
© BBC Worldwide Ltd 2001
Location photography by Craig Easton
© BBC Worldwide Ltd 2001
Commissioning Editor: Nicky Copeland
Project Editor: Rachel Copus
Cover Art Director: Pene Parker
Book Art Director: Sarah Ponder
Designer: Susannah Good
Food stylist: Silvana Franco
assisted by Sharon Hearne and Nicola Kelly
Food stylists for location photographs: Jenny White and Clare Lewis
Props stylist: Penny Markham

This book is published to accompany the television series
Gourmet Express 2 which was first broadcast in 2001.
The series was produced by BBC Birmingham.
Executive Producer: Nick Vaughan-Barratt
Series Producer: Sara Kozak
Director: Stuart Bateup

This book is available at special discounts for bulk purchases by groups or organizations for sales promotions, premiums, fundraising and educational purposes. For details, contact: Stewart House Publishing Inc., Special Sales Department, 195 Allstate Parkway, Markham, Ontario L3R 4T8. Toll free 1-866-474-3478.

1 2 3 4 5 6   07 06 05 04 03 02

All the spoon measurements in this book are level unless otherwise stated. A tablespoon is 15 ml; a teaspoon is 5 ml. Follow one set of measurements when preparing any of the recipes. Do not mix metric with imperial. All eggs used in the recipes are medium sized. All vegetables should be peeled unless the recipe says otherwise.

CONTENTS

INTRODUCTION

Welcome to my second *Gourmet Express* book.

What a thrill it's been writing, testing and eating my way through it. I thought at first it would be really difficult to come up with another 100 recipes that are easy to prepare, fit in with modern living, look appetizing and taste fantastic. Well, once I started, there was no stopping me – or my friends, who were immediately either on the phone looking for a dinner date or, more to the point, knocking on the door uninvited saying, 'we were just passing by'. It's been a real pleasure entertaining them and, of course, you get an instant reaction to the food – y'know, 'hmmm, lovely', 'ooohhh, that's gorgeous', or 'Ains, this is wicked!' It's always nice to be complimented on your food; it gives you a real buzz. Besides, it's not everyday someone says, 'well done', unless you've just passed your driving test.

There was the odd recipe that didn't make the final cut, but what you have here is the best, and once you have experienced the wonderful delights on offer in *Gourmet Express 2* you'll realize how accessible great food can be. I've taken on board food from all over the world to produce a collection of exciting recipes. From Europe we have: Smoked Bacon and Dolcelatte Risotto from Italy; Lightning Lamb Cassoulet and One-pot Chunky Beef Bourguignonne from France; Cracked Tapas Patatas Bravas, Spain; Portuguese String-tied, Stuffed Sardines; and Mama's Greek Butter-bean Salad, to name but a few. There's also a delightful, succulent Lamb Shank Rogan Josh from India, Sesame-salt Roast Sea bass with Ginger Soy Dressing (very much a Chinese influence here), Spicy Thai Beef Salad, as well as a few classics from our own back garden … and the desserts are to die for.

This book has been written to get you into the kitchen, cooking and producing stunning meals with the least amount of fuss, creating dishes that don't compromise on flavour or style. Whether you're standing with a plate full of grub, fork in your hand, watching the television, lazing on the sofa with a delicious bowl of pasta and catching up on the new CD, feeding the family at the dining table, or having friends around for supper, you'll always find something to titillate those taste buds.

Now, before we even start, here's a little something to get you going and give you lots of confidence. After a mouthful of these you'll be on your way to lots of tasty, time-saving meals without all the fuss. **Spoon Crab Canapés**, the perfect way to begin a casual dinner party.

To make enough canapés for six people, all you need to do is mix together 150 g (5 oz) fresh or canned white crabmeat, with 2 chopped green onions, ¼ teaspoon cayenne pepper and 2 tablespoons crème fraîche. Add a little salt and pepper and a squeeze of lemon juice to taste and chill the mixture until you're ready to serve. When your guests are about to arrive, divide the crab mixture between 12 teaspoons, then top each one with a spot of sweet chili sauce and a chervil leaf. Arrange on a platter and serve. What could be easier than that?

Have fun … it's only food, so enjoy the experience. Happy, smelly cooking!

Love

CHAPTER ONE SNACKS & BRUNCH

Toasted halloumi cheese and chorizo skewers

Halloumi is a great cheese for grilling because it holds its shape when warmed and has a wonderful texture. It's now readily available from larger supermarkets, sometimes packed in water for freshness – make sure you drain it thoroughly and rinse it before use. To enjoy these delicious skewers at their best, make sure you eat them hot as they become quite chewy when cold.

PREPARATION: 20 minutes COOKING TIME: 10 minutes

SERVES 4

1 loaf flavored focaccia (see Chef's Tip below)

70 g pack thin-cut chorizo

10 fresh basil leaves

250 g (9 oz) halloumi

2 tablespoons chili oil

1 lemon, cut into wedges, to serve

METHOD

1 Halve the focaccia horizontally then arrange the chorizo slices, overlapping, across the base of the sandwich. Place the basil leaves on the chorizo then sandwich the bread back together. Using a serrated knife cut the sandwich into about 40 2.5 cm (1 inch) squares.

2 Cut the halloumi in half lengthways to make 2 long blocks roughly 2.5 cm (1 inch) thick. Now slice each block thinly to give a total of 32 square slices of cheese. Thread the halloumi and sandwich squares alternately on to 8 bamboo skewers, starting and ending each stick with a sandwich. Brush lightly with the chili oil.

3 Heat a ridged grill pan or heavy, non-stick frying-pan and cook the skewers for 2–3 minutes on each side until hot and golden brown. Serve garnished with lemon wedges.

CHEF'S TIP: A rectangular cheesy loaf measuring 13 x 20 cm (5 x 8 inches) is the perfect size for this recipe. If you have a round or oval loaf it doesn't matter – if some of the edges of the sandwiches are rounded or some squares are smaller than others, it all adds to the charm of the skewers. And if the cheese breaks or is uneven, thread it on – it'll still look great. Enjoy!

Toasted halloumi cheese and chorizo skewers

Black and blue Cajun-chicken sandwich

An American classic made in heaven.

PREPARATION: 10 minutes COOKING TIME: 10 minutes

SERVES 2

1 large skinless, boneless chicken breast, about 150 g (5 oz)

1 tablespoon all-purpose flour

1 teaspoon cayenne

1 teaspoon ground mixed spice (mixture of allspice, cinnamon, nutmeg,

ginger, coriander and cloves)

½ teaspoon dried oregano

1–2 tablespoons vegetable oil for shallow-frying

4 thick slices crusty bread

2 tablespoons mayonnaise

¼ cucumber

salt and freshly ground black pepper

75 g (½ cup) blue cheese such as Gorgonzola or Stilton

METHOD

1 Cut the chicken breast in half horizontally. Place between two sheets of plastic wrap and flatten with a rolling pin until 1 cm (½ inch) thick. Mix together the flour, cayenne, mixed spice, oregano, salt and pepper. Dust the chicken in the seasoned flour, shaking off any excess.

2 Heat the oil in a large frying-pan and cook the chicken for 5 minutes on each side until well browned and a little charred around the edges.

3 Meanwhile, toast the bread and spread two of the slices with mayonnaise. Thinly slice the cucumber and arrange over the mayonnaise. Place a piece of chicken on each, crumble over the blue cheese and top with the remaining slices of toast. Cut in half and serve warm.

CHEF'S TIP: You can make this dish more of a meal by serving the sandwich open with an arugula salad on the side.

Pancetta hash browns

Hash browns are an irresistible addition to any cooked breakfast. These crispy bacon wedges make an excellent snack in their own right and, when topped with a fried egg, a tasty breakfast treat.

PREPARATION: 20 minutes COOKING TIME: 15 minutes

SERVES 4

4 small floury potatoes, about 100 g (4 oz) each

75 g (3 oz) thin-sliced pancetta, roughly chopped

2 green onions, thinly sliced

salt and freshly ground black pepper

METHOD

1 Cook the potatoes whole in a pan of boiling water for 15 minutes until just tender – don't worry if they're a little hard in the center.

2 Heat a large, non-stick frying-pan and cook the pancetta for 2–3 minutes until golden. Remove with a slotted spoon and drain on paper towel.

3 Coarsely grate the potatoes, including the skin, into a large bowl, then stir in the pancetta, green onions and some salt and pepper.

4 Return the mixture to the frying-pan and cook for 8 minutes until golden. Carefully turn the hash on to a large plate, then turn it over and slide back into the pan, so that the cooked side is facing up. Cook for a further 5 minutes until crisp and golden brown. Cut into wedges and serve warm.

CHEF'S TIP: For a quick fishy alternative, replace the pancetta with a small tin of cooked salmon. Simply drain it, flake it up and add to the grated potato with the green onions and the salt and pepper.

Baconeese corn muffins

These muffins make a super breakfast served warm from the oven with a dollop of butter or soft cheese, or wrapped in a paper napkin and eaten on the go.

PREPARATION: 15 minutes COOKING TIME: 20 minutes

MAKES 8

100 g (4 oz) strip bacon, roughly chopped

50 g (¾ cup) butter

300 g (1⅔ cups) all-purpose flour

2 teaspoons baking powder

25g (2 tablespoons) cornmeal

1 teaspoon fine granulated sugar

1 teaspoon salt

120 g (4½ oz) Cheddar, finely diced

1 egg, beaten

300 ml (1 cup) milk

METHOD

1 Pre-heat the oven to 200°C/400°F/Gas 6. Line a muffin tin with paper cases, or cut parchment into 8 x 15 cm (6 inch) circles and push them into the tin.

2 Cook the bacon in a non-stick frying-pan for 3–4 minutes until golden. Drain on paper towel. Add the butter to the pan, remove from the heat and leave to melt.

3 Sift the flour and baking powder into a large bowl and stir in the cornmeal, sugar, salt, cooked bacon and three quarters of the cheese. Crack the egg into a separate bowl and whisk in the milk and melted butter.

4 Stir the liquid into the dry ingredients, taking care not to over-mix. Divide the mixture between the paper cases, scatter over the reserved cheese and bake for 20 minutes or so until well risen and just firm.

5 Transfer to a wire rack, and allow to cool slightly – if you can wait, that is.

Baconeese corn muffins

Pesto-rippled scrambled eggs

This is absolutely delicious, and the rippled effect comes not only from the pesto, but also from the egg yolks and whites being mixed together. But, be warned, it's worth sharing the finished dish with your partner as it contains raw garlic, which can have quite a long-lasting effect.

PREPARATION: 15 minutes COOKING TIME: 5 minutes

SERVES 2

1 small garlic clove, roughly chopped

1 tablespoon toasted pine nuts

1 handful of fresh basil

1 tablespoon freshly grated Parmesan, plus extra to serve

2–3 tablespoons olive oil

1–2 tablespoons of butter

4 large eggs

salt and freshly ground black pepper

hot, buttered, toasted bread or bagels, to serve

METHOD

1 Place the garlic and pine nuts in a mini food processor and blitz until finely chopped. Add the basil and Parmesan and blitz again until well blended. Add the oil and some salt and pepper and pulse until well combined.

2 Heat the butter in a small pan and crack in the eggs, season, then leave to set for 2 minutes. With a wooden spoon, stir very gently so the eggs begin to set in clumps of white and yellow. Before the eggs have completely set, lightly stir in the pesto.

3 Pile on to the hot toast or bagels, scatter over the Parmesan and serve immediately.

Portabello mushroom open-top toast

Portabello mushrooms have a great firm texture and full flavor, making them ideal for cooking and pairing with other flavorsome ingredients such as garlicky soft cheese. Great for brunch – even better as a late-night snack.

PREPARATION: 10 minutes COOKING TIME: 10 minutes

SERVES 2

1 tablespoon olive oil

4 large Portabello mushrooms, about 50 g (2 oz) each

6 cherry tomatoes, halved

1 x 80 g pack garlic and herb soft cheese

salt and freshly ground black pepper

2 thick slices of hot, buttered toast, to serve

chives, to garnish

METHOD

1 Heat the oil in a large frying-pan, add the mushrooms, gill-side up and season lightly. Place 3 cherry tomato halves in each cap and dot over the soft cheese. Cook gently for 5 minutes over a low heat. Meanwhile, pre-heat the grill to medium.

2 Place the frying-pan under the grill for 2–3 minutes until the cheese is bubbling. Place two stuffed mushrooms on top of each slice of toast, garnish with chives and serve.

Portabello mushroom open-top toast

Posh French Toast BLT

For a quick snack or a truly indulgent breakfast, this is absolutely perfect – especially with a squirt of ketchup or brown sauce on the side.

PREPARATION: 10 minutes COOKING TIME: 10 minutes

SERVES 1

2 tablespoons olive oil

2 slices smoked back bacon

1 plum tomato, sliced lengthwise

1 large egg

2 tablespoons milk

2 slices white bread

small handful of watercress

1 tablespoon mayonnaise

salt and freshly ground black pepper

METHOD

1 Splash a little oil into a large, non-stick frying-pan. When hot, add the bacon and tomato slices. Cook over a high heat for a couple of minutes until the tomatoes are softened and a little browned and the bacon is done to your liking, then transfer to a plate. Remove the frying-pan from the heat and wipe clean with paper towel.

2 In a shallow bowl (I like to use a soup bowl) beat together the egg, milk and some salt and pepper.

3 Make a sandwich using the two slices of bread, add the bacon, tomato, watercress and mayonnaise. Press firmly together, then place the sandwich in the egg mixture. Leave for a few minutes, turning once or twice until all the egg mixture has been absorbed.

4 Add the remaining oil to the pan and return to the heat. Cook the sandwich for 3–4 minutes on each side until puffed and golden brown. Serve immediately.

Pineapple and coconut
smoothie

What a great way to start the day! If you don't have time to skin your pineapple, you can buy one ready prepared; it can save loads of time in the morning rush.

PREPARATION: 10 minutes

SERVES 2-4

1 medium pineapple

1 banana

1 x 200 ml carton coconut cream

METHOD

1 Cut the skin off the pineapple and discard, then roughly chop the flesh. Pass through an electric juicer.

2 Peel and mash the banana, then mix with a little of the coconut cream until smooth. Transfer to a large, ice-filled jug with the remaining coconut cream and the pineapple juice. Stir very well together until blended and frothy then pour into 4 chilled glasses and serve.

CHEF'S TIP: Try substituting a wedge of watermelon for the pineapple.

CHAPTER TWO SOUPS & STARTERS

Chorizo chowder

A warming, wintry soup, this makes a really satisfying supper or weekend lunch. Make sure you buy whole chorizo sausages and slice them yourself, as the packets of ready sliced chorizo that you can buy are too thin for this soup.

PREPARATION: 15 minutes COOKING TIME: 25 minutes

SERVES 4

1 tablespoon butter

1 small onion, finely chopped

4 garlic cloves, chopped

500 g (1 lb 2 oz) floury potatoes such as Maris Piper or King Edward, cubed

1 leek, thinly sliced

1 teaspoon cayenne

1 litre (4 cups) of vegetable stock

250 g (9 oz) chorizo sausage, cut into 1 cm (½ inch) wide slices, or 1 cm (½ inch) dice

salt and freshly ground black pepper

crusty bread, to serve

METHOD

1 Heat the butter in a large pan and cook the onion, garlic and potatoes for 5 minutes until lightly golden. Add the leek and cayenne and cook for a further 1 minute.

2 Add the stock, bring to the boil and simmer for 20 minutes until the potatoes are very soft and beginning to break up into the soup.

3 Using a potato masher, roughly mash the potatoes into the soup. Stir in the chorizo and simmer gently for 5 minutes until the orange-colored oil from the chorizo rises to the surface of the soup. Check the seasoning, ladle into bowls and garnish with a sprig of flat-leaf parsley. Serve with lots of crusty bread for mopping up.

Chorizo chowder

Chickpea, spinach and sweet potato soup

This is a lovely, hearty, warming soup that everyone adores, especially my veggie friends. Pair it with crusty bread for a cosy supper.

PREPARATION: 10 minutes COOKING TIME: 20 minutes

SERVES 4

2 tablespoons sunflower oil

1 onion, finely chopped

1 sweet potato, diced

1 garlic clove, thinly sliced

1 teaspoon cumin seeds

400 g can chickpeas, drained

2 tomatoes, roughly chopped

1 teaspoon honey

750 ml (2½ cups) hot vegetable stock

225 g (8 oz) baby spinach

salt and freshly ground black pepper

METHOD

1 Heat the oil in a large pan and cook the onion, sweet potato and garlic for 5 minutes, stirring until beginning to turn golden. Add the cumin seeds and cook for 30 seconds. Stir in the chickpeas, tomatoes and honey and cook for 1–2 minutes until the tomatoes begin to soften.

2 Stir in the hot stock, bring to the boil, then cover and simmer for 10 minutes until the sweet potato is tender.

3 Stir in the spinach and cook for 1 minute, stirring until the spinach wilts. Season to taste, then ladle into bowls and serve.

Hot Bloody Mary soup

The combination of tomato, vodka and chili works brilliantly in the classic cocktail and it's every bit as good in this dazzling soup – it certainly packs a punch. It's essential that you add the horseradish, sherry and vodka when the soup is off the boil, otherwise you'll impair the lovely flavor.

PREPARATION: 20 minutes COOKING TIME: 40 minutes

SERVES 4

1 kg (2¼ lb) ripe tomatoes, halved

2 red chilies, halved and seeded

2 teaspoons fine granulated sugar

2 tablespoons olive oil

750 ml (2½ cups) vegetable stock

1 tablespoon tomato paste

2 teaspoons horseradish sauce

2 tablespoons dry sherry

4 tablespoons vodka

4 small celery stalks, with leaves

celery salt, or salt and freshly ground black pepper

4 thin lemon slices, to garnish

METHOD

1 Pre-heat the oven to 200°C/400°F/Gas 4. Place the tomatoes cut-side up in a large roasting tin with the chilies and sprinkle over the sugar and some salt and pepper. Drizzle over the olive oil and roast for 30 minutes until softened and nicely browned.

2 Purée the roasted tomatoes in a blender with a little stock until smooth. For a really smooth soup, pass the purée through a sieve into a large pan, otherwise, transfer straight to the pan. Stir in the remaining stock and the tomato purée and heat gently through, without boiling.

3 Stir in the horseradish, sherry and vodka and check the seasoning. Place a celery stalk in each of four bowls and ladle over the soup. Grind over black pepper, float a slice of lemon on each and serve.

Asian salmon laksa

This Asian soup is substantial enough to serve as a smart supper, but is also lovely as a dinner-party starter, providing it's not followed by too heavy a main course. I like to use bok choy, but you could use spinach.

PREPARATION: 20 minutes COOKING TIME: 10 minutes

SERVES 4

300 g (11 oz) salmon fillet

juice of 2 limes

100 g (4 oz) rice noodles

1 tablespoon vegetable oil

2.5 cm (1 inch) piece ginger root, finely chopped

2 garlic cloves, finely chopped

1 shallot, finely chopped

450 ml (1½ cups) hot vegetable stock

1¾ cups coconut milk

1 lemon grass stalk

2 teaspoons Thai red curry paste

200 g (7 oz) bok choy, halved or quartered if large

1 tablespoon soy sauce

1 small red chili, sliced to garnish

METHOD

1 Boil a kettle of water. Cut the salmon widthways into 1-cm (½-inch) wide slices (you should get roughly 12 slices out of a fillet of this size). Place in a bowl and squeeze over the lime juice; set aside for 20 minutes.

2 Meanwhile, place the noodles in a large bowl, cover with the boiling water and set aside.

3 Heat the oil in a large pan or wok, throw in the ginger, garlic and shallots and cook for 3–4 minutes until softened. Pour in the stock and coconut milk, then bruise the lemon grass stalk with a rolling pin – a quick bash or two should do it – and add to the pan with the curry paste. Stir well. Then, bring the soup to the boil, reduce the heat and simmer very gently for 5 minutes.

4 Add the salmon, bok choy and soy sauce and simmer for another 2–3 minutes until the bok choy is tender, but still crunchy.

5 Drain the noodles and divide between four bowls. Ladle over the soup, then float a chili ring or two in each bowl. Serve immediately.

Shredded chicken
and lemon grass soup

This is a low-fat, delicate, aromatic broth. It makes a lovely light supper or can serve up to six as a starter. For this soup I use the whole chili, including the seeds, which, when blended with the other flavors, gives it a wonderful kick. Make sure you use whole thighs with the bones in as this contributes greatly to the flavor of the broth.

PREPARATION: 10 minutes COOKING TIME: 35 minutes

SERVES 4

6 whole chicken thighs

2 lemon grass stalks

2 kaffir lime leaves

2 garlic cloves, halved

1 red chili, roughly chopped

4 cm (1½ inch) piece ginger root, thickly sliced

juice of 1 lime

4 tablespoons light soy sauce

1 bunch green onions, thinly sliced

1 tablespoon fresh coriander leaves

METHOD

1 Remove the skin from the chicken thighs and discard; place the thighs in a large pan. Bruise the lemon grass with a rolling pin and crumple the lime leaves in the palm of your hand. Place in the pan with the garlic, chili, including the seeds, and ginger and 1.5 litres (2½ pints) water. Bring to the boil and simmer for 30 minutes until the chicken is cooked right through.

2 Strain the stock into a clean pan then, using 2 forks, shred the meat off the bones. Return the chicken to the pan with the fresh lime juice, soy sauce and sliced green onions. Heat through gently and, when steaming hot, ladle into bowls. Loosely scatter over the coriander leaves and serve.

CHEF'S TIP: This soup is naturally quite low in fat, but for pretty presentation and a little extra flavour, try drizzling a splash of chili or sesame oil over the surface of each serving.

Curried parsnip soup

I like to serve this soup with those delicious root-vegetable chips you can buy now. Just drop a handful into the center of each bowlful.

PREPARATION: 15 minutes COOKING TIME: 45 minutes

SERVES 6

4 large parsnips, cubed, about 750 g (2½ cups)

6 whole garlic cloves, skinned

4 cm (1½ inch) piece ginger root, roughly chopped

1 tablespoon vegetable oil

1.2 litres (4 cups) hot vegetable stock

400 ml can coconut milk

1 tablespoon Thai red curry paste

salt and freshly ground black pepper

1 tablespoon chopped fresh coriander

root vegetable chips, to serve

METHOD

1 Pre-heat the oven to 200°C/400°F/Gas 6. Place the parsnips, garlic and ginger in a large, deep roasting pan, drizzle over the oil, season with salt and pepper and roast for 20 minutes until golden.

2 Pour in half the stock, the coconut milk and curry paste and return to the oven for a further 20 minutes until the vegetables are tender.

3 Transfer to a blender and blend until creamy and smooth. Add the remaining hot stock and the coriander and check the seasoning. Ladle into warm bowls and serve with the root vegetable chips.

CHEF'S TIP: This soup is served warm but not piping hot. If you prefer, it can be warmed through a little further in a pan on the stove before serving. It can also be chilled and gently reheated for serving later.

Chinese crisp-fried salt-and-pepper squid

This is one of my all-time favorite Chinese dishes and it's surprisingly easy to make. I think baby squid are best for this recipe as they cook quickly and are lovely and tender. Baby squid can be bought from larger supermarkets, or try your local fishmonger – if you ask him nicely he might score them for you, too.

PREPARATION: 15 minutes COOKING TIME: 10 minutes

SERVES 4

300 g (11 oz) young squid, each about 4–6 cm (1¾–2½ inches) long, cleaned

vegetable oil for deep-frying

1 tablespoon sea salt

1 tablespoon black peppercorns

75 g (⅓ cup) cornstarch

1 red chili, very thinly sliced, seeds and all

2 green onions, cut into 1 cm (½ inch) pieces

soy sauce and lemon wedges, to serve

METHOD

1 Slit each squid body open along one side with a sharp knife then score the inside of each in a criss-cross pattern. Set aside with the tentacles.

2 Heat 5 cm (2 inches) of vegetable oil in the base of a wok or deep frying-pan.

3 Place the sea salt and peppercorns in a pestle and mortar and crush coarsely together. Stir into the cornstarch, then toss with the squid to coat – you might find it easier to place the ingredients in a large plastic bag and shake well together.

4 Cook the chilies and green onions in the hot oil for 30 seconds then scoop them out with a mesh spoon and drain on kitchen paper. Cook the squid body and tentacles in the pan for 2 minutes until it rolls up and turns crisp and lightly golden – you may need to do this in batches so the oil stays hot. Drain on kitchen paper.

5 Transfer the squid to a plate, scatter over the crispy chili and green onions and serve with soy sauce for drizzling and lemon wedges for squeezing over.

Chinese crisp-fried salt-and-pepper squid

Crispy noodle-wrapped shrimp
with rice-wine dipping sauce

This is a very stylish starter. It's ideal for a dinner party menu, followed by Warm Oriental Duck and Mango Salad (page 78) then Srikhand with Iced Mango Shards (page 137). Try to get your shrimp from a Chinese grocer or a local fishmonger, as the ones in the supermarket are often too small for this dish.

PREPARATION: 20 minutes COOKING TIME: 10 minutes

SERVES 4

75 g (3 oz) dried, fine, Chinese egg noodles

1 small mango, skinned, pitted and thinly sliced

12 large, raw, shell-on, headless shrimp, each about 8 cm (3¼ inches) long

salt

vegetable oil for deep frying

FOR THE DIPPING SAUCE

5 tablespoons rice or white wine vinegar

3 tablespoons fine granulated sugar

1 red bird's-eye chili, very thinly sliced, seeds and all

sprigs of fresh coriander and wedges of lime, to serve

METHOD

1 Begin by making the dipping sauce: place the vinegar and sugar in a small pan and bring to the boil, stirring until the sugar dissolves. Remove from the heat, add the sliced chili and leave to cool completely. If you want to get ahead, the sauce can be made a day or two before you need it, then kept covered in the fridge.

2 Cook the egg noodles in a pan of boiling water according to packet instructions. Drain well, then cool in cold water and drain again. Gently heat 5 cm (2 inches) of oil in a deep pan.

3 Shell the shrimp, leaving the tail section intact. Pass a short bamboo skewer through the shrimp from top to tail. Place a slice of mango on each shrimp and season with a little salt. Gather about 6 strands of noodle and wrap them around the shrimp to secure together the shrimp and the mango. Repeat to make 12 shrimp sticks.

4 Test the oil temperature with a piece of noodle: it should turn crisp and golden in about 1 minute. Cook the shrimp in batches for 2–3 minutes until the noodles are crisp and the shrimp pink. Drain on paper towel and serve hot with small bowls of the dipping sauce. You may choose to slide the shrimp off the sticks before serving, or leave them on. Decorate with sprigs of coriander and wedges of lime, to serve.

Crispy noodle-wrapped shrimp with rice-wine dipping sauce

Seared scallops with
endive and Roquefort

If you enjoy seafood that's rich and delicious, this is undoubtedly one of the finest dishes on offer. I always think Queen scallops work best in this dish – your fishmonger should be able to get them for you. If you're daunted by the prospect of cleaning them, your fishmonger will probably do this for you too.

PREPARATION: 10 minutes COOKING TIME: 5 minutes

SERVES 4

2 small heads Belgian endive

12 small scallops, shelled

2 tablespoons olive oil

1 teaspoon walnut oil

juice of half a lime

100 g (4 oz) Roquefort, crumbled into 1 cm (½ inch) pieces

2 tablespoons snipped fresh chives

salt and freshly ground black pepper

METHOD

1 Break open the endive and place 3 leaves on each of 4 plates.

2 Brush the scallops with a little of the olive oil. Cook in a hot, non-stick frying-pan for 1 minute on each side until golden.

3 Place a scallop on each leaf. Whisk together the remaining olive oil, walnut oil, lime juice and some salt and pepper. Top each leaf with a cube or two of Roquefort and a scattering of chives, then drizzle over the dressing and serve while the scallops are still just warm.

Vietnamese-style pork
in lettuce-leaf cups

Now, here's a classic Oriental dish that's surprisingly easy to make at home. What's even better is that you can prepare it the day before and then, just before your guests arrive, assemble the dish in a matter of minutes. It's perfect to serve up for a dinner party, or just to enjoy with the family.

PREPARATION: 15 minutes + cooling time COOKING TIME: 10 minutes

SERVES 4

1 tablespoon vegetable oil

1 shallot, finely chopped

2 garlic cloves, finely chopped

1 red chili, seeded and finely chopped

250 g (1 cup) minced pork

1 teaspoon Chinese five spice

220 g can water chestnuts, drained and chopped

1 tablespoon Thai fish sauce (nam pla)

2 tablespoons light soy sauce

1 tablespoon clear honey

2 Little Gem lettuce hearts (or hearts of romaine)

75 g (½ cup) bean sprouts

fresh coriander leaves, to garnish

METHOD

1 Heat the oil in a large pan and cook the shallot and garlic for 2 minutes. Add the chili, pork and five spice and cook for a further 5 minutes. Stir in the water chestnuts, fish sauce, soy sauce and honey and warm through gently, stirring until the pork is cooked through. Allow to cool then chill for at least 20 minutes.

2 Separate the lettuce leaves and place 12 on a large serving platter. Stir the bean sprouts into the minced pork then spoon into the lettuce leaves. Garnish with coriander leaves and serve.

Crispy Prosciutto
and asparagus salad

This is a gorgeous main-meal salad. When in season, during May, try to use delicious home-grown English asparagus.

PREPARATION: 10 minutes COOKING TIME: 20 minutes

SERVES 4

6 eggs

250 g (9 oz) asparagus

25 g (2 tablespoons) butter

squeeze of fresh lemon juice

8 slices prosciutto, about 85 g (3¼ oz)

salt and freshly ground black pepper

Parmesan shavings, to serve

METHOD

1 Cook the eggs in a pan of boiling water for exactly 8 minutes. Sit a steamer or colander over the eggs, put in the asparagus, cover and cook for 4–5 minutes until just tender – alternatively, cook in a pan of boiling water for 2–3 minutes.

2 Drain the eggs and asparagus and cool under cold water.

3 Melt the butter in a small pan then, with a wire whisk, beat in some lemon juice and salt and pepper to taste.

4 Heat a ridged grill pan or heavy, non-stick frying-pan. Cook the slices of ham, two at a time in the hot pan for 30 seconds on each side. Set aside on paper towel. Cook the asparagus in the hot pan (making good use of the fat left from the ham) for 2–3 minutes to give light bar-marks.

5 Shell and halve the eggs and arrange on four plates with the asparagus, topped with the crispy ham. Drizzle over the lemon-butter dressing. Scatter over the shaved Parmesan and top with a good grind of black pepper. A glass or two of chilled white wine is the perfect accompaniment to this dish.

Crispy Prosciutto and asparagus salad

Beef satay chili sticks

These tasty morsels are the perfect way to start off a dinner party or to serve with drinks – they're never around for very long. I like to hand them round to my friends when we're watching football on TV.

PREPARATION: 15 minutes + marinating time COOKING TIME: 5 minutes

SERVES 4

500 g (1 lb 2 oz) trimmed 2.5 cm (1 inch) sirloin steak

4 tablespoons light soy sauce

2 teaspoons brown sugar

1 teaspoon vinegar

coriander leaves or shredded green onions, to garnish

FOR THE SAUCE

½ cup dry-roasted peanuts

1 garlic clove

200 ml carton coconut cream

juice of 1 lime

1 tablespoon light soy sauce

pinch of crushed chilli flakes

METHOD

1 You will need 8 bamboo skewers for this recipe. Before you start, soak them in hot water for approximately 20 minutes.

2 Slice the steak lengthwise into 5 mm (¼ inch) thick strips. When you lay them flat, they will be 2.5 cm (1 inch) wide and about 12 cm (4¾ inches) long, depending upon the length of your steak. Place the steak strips into a bowl with the soy sauce, sugar and vinegar. Stir well together and leave to marinate for at least 15 minutes and up to 2 hours.

3 Meanwhile, make the satay sauce: place the peanuts and garlic in a food processor and whizz until very finely chopped. Add the coconut cream and whizz again until well blended. Pour into a small pan and heat gently for 3–4 minutes until the sauce darkens and thickens slightly. Add the soy sauce and lime juice to taste, then remove from the heat.

4 Thread the steak on to the bamboo skewers – make a concertina with each strip so that the skewer passes through several times – and place on a foil-lined baking sheet. Cook under a hot grill for 2–3 minutes on each side until browned but still pink in the centre. You can cook them for longer if you like your steak better done.

5 Pour the warm satay sauce into a serving bowl and sprinkle with the crushed chilies. Arrange the beef sticks on a platter, garnish with coriander or green onions and serve with the sauce for dipping.

Quick chicken liver and
tarragon paté

Forget about paté that takes ages to cook in a water bath. This recipe is incredibly simple and tastes fabulous. Just cook, purée, set and serve. It's as easy as that!

PREPARATION: 20 minutes + chilling time   COOKING TIME: 10 minutes

SERVES 6

150 g (¾ cup) butter, at room temperature

225 g (8 oz) chicken livers

2 tablespoons brandy

2 garlic cloves, roughly chopped

1 tablespoon chopped fresh tarragon

⅔ cup heavy cream

salt and freshly ground black pepper

hot, buttered toast, to serve

TO GARNISH

50 g (4 tablespoons) butter

12 fresh tarragon leaves

METHOD

1 Melt a large spoonful of the butter in a large frying-pan and cook the chicken livers for 3–4 minutes on each side until well browned but still slightly pink in the center.

2 Place in a food processor and whizz until smooth. Remove the pan from the heat, add the brandy and swirl round to gather up the pan juices. Add to the food processor with the garlic, tarragon and the remaining butter and whizz again until well blended.

3 Add some salt and pepper followed by the cream and process again until well mixed. Spoon into 6 ramekins, smoothing the surface level, and leave to cool completely.

4 To finish off, melt the butter and pour over the surface of the paté. Drop in a few tarragon leaves as decoration.

5 Cover with plastic wrap and chill for at least a few hours, but up to a day or two. Serve straight from the fridge with hot, buttered toast, or melba toast if you're feeling posh.

CHAPTER THREE THE MAIN COURSE

Chili crab linguine with vodka

A delicious, delicate dish this, I often serve it up as a simple supper for my wife Clare and myself, once the kids are tucked in bed. I tend to use canned crab, but if you can get fresh, all the better. If you are feeding youngsters, skip the chili and the vodka, but I'd recommend that you keep this dish strictly for adults.

PREPARATION: 10 minutes COOKING TIME: 15 minutes

SERVES 2

175 g (6 oz) dried linguine

1 tablespoon olive oil

1 shallot, finely chopped

1 small garlic clove, finely chopped

1 red chili, seeded and finely chopped

2 ripe tomatoes, roughly chopped

1 tablespoon vodka (optional)

170 g can white crab meat, drained

2 tablespoons chopped fresh flat-leaf parsley

salt and freshly ground black pepper

METHOD

1 Cook the pasta in a large pan of boiling, salted water according to packet instructions.

2 Meanwhile, heat the olive oil in a frying-pan and cook the shallot, garlic and chili over a low to medium heat for 2–3 minutes until beginning to soften, but not brown. Add the tomatoes, increase the heat and cook for 4–5 minutes until pulpy.

3 Now stir in the vodka, if using, followed by the crab meat, and stir gently together. Season to taste.

4 Drain the pasta well and return to the pan. Add the sauce and the chopped parsley and stir loosely together. Divide between bowls and top with a good grinding of black pepper.

CHEF'S TIP: Don't be tempted to get out the Parmesan – it really doesn't suit the flavor of the crab.

Chili crab linguine with vodka

Grilled mackerel
with shallot and coriander pickle

Mackerel is a lovely oily fish and its flavor contrasts wonderfully with the sharpness of the quick pickle that's served with it. I cook these under the grill, but they're even more fabulous cooked alfresco over hot coals in the great outdoors. I like to serve this with Spice-roasted Butternut Squash (page 129) and a simple green salad.

PREPARATION: 10 minutes + marinating time COOKING TIME: 10 minutes

SERVES 4

4 x 300–350 g (11–12 oz) whole, cleaned mackerel

1 tablespoon olive oil

sea salt and coarsely ground black pepper

FOR THE PICKLE

2 shallots

2 cornichons or small pickled gherkins

4 tablespoons red wine vinegar

3 tablespoons fine granulated sugar

¼ teaspoon table salt

1 teaspoon yellow mustard seeds

1 tablespoon fresh coriander, roughly chopped

METHOD

1 Begin by making the pickle: halve and peel the shallots, then slice them lengthwise as thinly as possible. Thinly slice the cornichons and place in a bowl with the shallots, vinegar, sugar, salt and mustard seeds. Set aside for 20 minutes.

2 Meanwhile, diagonally cut 3 deep slashes on each side of the fish. Smear with the olive oil then season with salt and pepper. Heat the grill to medium. Place the fish on a foil-lined baking sheet and cook under the grill for 4–5 minutes on each side until the skin is crisp and brown and the flesh is cooked.

3 Stir the coriander leaves into the shallot mixture and leave for 2–3 minutes. Transfer the mackerel to serving plates and spoon over the pickle.

CHEF'S TIP: Crusty fresh bread would be ideal to serve with this, so that you can mop up all those juices.

Gruyère cracker-crusted haddock

The crackers add a fantastic crunch to this tasty fish dish.

PREPARATION: 10 minutes COOKING TIME: 10 minutes

SERVES 4

75 g (3 oz) water crackers or cream crackers

75 g (½ cup) finely grated Gruyère

½ teaspoon cayenne

2 tablespoons chopped fresh parsley

2 tablespoons olive oil

4 x 150 g (5 oz) skinless, boneless haddock fillets

salt and freshly ground black pepper

METHOD

1 Crumble the crackers into a food processor with the Gruyère, cayenne and parsley and blitz until well blended. Add 1 tablespoon of the olive oil and some seasoning and pulse again until well blended.

2 Heat the remaining oil in a large frying-pan and cook the haddock for 2–3 minutes until nearly cooked through. Sprinkle the cracker-crumb mixture over the top of the fillets, pressing down firmly with the fingertips.

3 Pre-heat the grill to medium. Place the pan under the grill for 4–5 minutes until the fish is completely cooked through and the crumb topping is golden brown.

CHEF'S TIP: Gruyère has a full flavor and stretchy quality when melted. It can be substituted in this dish with tasty Jarlsberg or milder Emmenthal.

Smoked haddock, leek and rösti-pot pie

Haddock and leeks make a wonderful flavor combination and they're finished off beautifully with a crunchy potato and Cheddar cheese topping.

PREPARATION: 25 minutes COOKING TIME: 25 minutes

SERVES 4-6

500 g (1 lb 2 oz) smoked haddock fillet

300 ml (1 cup) milk

25 g (2 tablespoons) butter

2 large leeks, sliced

25 g (2 tablespoons) all-purpose flour

2 teaspoons wholegrain mustard

1 cup mascarpone

3 hard boiled eggs, quartered

1 large potato, about 250 g (9 oz), such as Maris Piper or King Edward

75 g (½ cup) coarsely grated old Cheddar

salt and freshly ground black pepper

METHOD

1 Place the fish in a heatproof dish. Bring the milk to the boil in a small pan and pour over the fish; set aside for 5 minutes.

2 Pre-heat the oven to 200°C/400°F/Gas 6. Heat the butter in a large pan and cook the sliced leeks for 3 minutes until softened. Stir in the flour and cook for 1 minute, stirring continuously. Strain the milk from the fish into the pan and stir well.

3 Bring to a boil and continue stirring until thickened. Now add the mustard and mascarpone, mixing until warmed through and well blended. Add salt and pepper to taste and remove from the heat.

4 Skin the fish, then cut or break the flesh into chunks and transfer to a 2 litre (3½ pint) heatproof dish. Add the quartered eggs, then pour over the leek sauce, stirring lightly to mix everything together.

5 Peel then coarsely grate the potato and mix with the cheese and some freshly ground black pepper. Scatter this mixture evenly over the top of the pie then bake for 25–30 minutes until the topping is golden brown. Serve straight from the oven.

CHEF'S TIP: The potato will turn grey when exposed to the air so make sure you grate it at the last minute and bake the pie as soon as the topping is on.

Portuguese string-tied, stuffed sardines

Ask your fishmonger to bone the sardines for you while keeping them whole – it's very easy to do. Simply serve with a plain salad for a lovely summery supper or lunch.

PREPARATION: 20 minutes COOKING TIME: 10 minutes

SERVES 4

2 tablespoons olive oil

1 shallot, finely chopped

2 garlic cloves, finely chopped

1 teaspoon chopped capers

4 tablespoons chopped fresh parsley

100 g (½ cup) fresh white breadcrumbs

grated rind and juice of 1 lemon

12 x 50–75 g (2–3 oz) whole sardines, boned if possible

3 mild red chilies, quartered lengthwise and seeded

salt and freshly ground black pepper

METHOD

1 Heat 1 tablespoon of the oil in a large pan and cook the shallot and garlic for 4–5 minutes until softened and golden. Stir in the capers, parsley, breadcrumbs, lemon rind and juice and some salt and pepper.

2 Open out the sardines and place a tablespoon of the stuffing mixture into each cavity. Close the sardines to enclose the filling, then tie with string to secure.

3 Pre-heat the grill to high. Slip a strip of chili under the strings of each fish then brush with a little olive oil. Season with salt and pepper then cook under the grill or in a non-stick frying-pan for 3–4 minutes on each side until cooked through and a little charred. Serve warm with salad.

Sesame-salt roast sea bass
with ginger soy dressing

This is a really glamorous and colorful dish. Apart from some careful chopping, it's really easy to prepare. Serve it with my Simple Wok Noodles (page 133).

PREPARATION: 15 minutes COOKING TIME: 30 minutes

SERVES 4

2 tablespoons sesame seeds

2 teaspoons sea salt

1 sea bass, about 1.25–1.5kg (2¾–3¼ lb)

1–2 tablespoons sunflower oil

2 cm (¾ inch) piece ginger root, shredded

1 garlic clove, finely chopped

1 red chili, seeded and shredded

4 tablespoons soy sauce

2 teaspoons white vinegar or rice vinegar

2 teaspoons sesame oil

4 green onions, shredded

handful of fresh coriander

salt and freshly ground black pepper

lime wedges, to serve

METHOD

1 Pre-heat the oven to 200°C/400°F/Gas 6. Mix together the sesame seeds and salt. Season the cavity of the fish then make 3 diagonal slashes across each side of the bass so it cooks evenly.

2 Transfer the fish to a large roasting tin and brush with a little oil. Sprinkle with sesame salt and roast for 25–30 minutes until the fish is cooked and lightly golden.

3 Meanwhile, splash a little sunflower oil into a small pan and cook the ginger, garlic and chilli for 2 minutes, without browning. Add the soy sauce, vinegar and sesame oil and remove from the heat.

4 When the fish is cooked, transfer to a large serving platter. Pour over the ginger dressing, then scatter over the green onions and coriander leaves. Serve immediately with lime wedges for squeezing over.

Sesame-salt roast sea bass with ginger soy dressing

Cold poached salmon
with cucumber and crème fraîche sauce

This is a really simple but very elegant summer dish. It's light and healthy, so I choose to use low-fat crème fraîche for the sauce. Serve with boiled, new, Jersey potatoes.

PREPARATION: 15 minutes + cooling time COOKING TIME: 5 minutes

SERVES 4

4 peppercorns

6 fresh dill sprigs, plus extra to serve

1 lemon, thinly sliced

450 ml (1½ cups) boiling water

4 x 175 g (6 oz) salmon fillets

FOR THE SAUCE

1 mini cucumber, roughly chopped

2 fresh dill sprigs

200 ml carton low-fat crème fraîche, or low-fat yogurt

salt and freshly ground black pepper

METHOD

1 Place the peppercorns, dill and four lemon slices (reserve the remaining slices for the garnish) in a large sauté pan and pour in the boiling water. Add the salmon, cover with a tight-fitting lid and cook for 5 minutes. Turn off the heat and leave the salmon to cool completely in the water – this should cook it perfectly. Remove from the pan then transfer to a plate, cover and chill until ready to serve.

2 To make the sauce, place the cucumber and dill in a food processor and whizz until smooth. Add the crème fraîche or yogurt and some salt and pepper and pulse to make a smooth, pourable sauce.

3 To serve, place a salmon fillet on 4 plates and pour over the sauce. Garnish each with a slice of lemon and sprig of dill.

Souffléd smoked salmon
and tarragon omelette

This delicious soufflette makes a lovely main course for one or a posh breakfast for two – beats boring old scrambled eggs and smoked salmon hands down.

PREPARATION: 10 minutes COOKING TIME: 7 minutes

SERVES 1

3 eggs, separated

1 small garlic clove, crushed

1 tablespoon chopped fresh tarragon, plus a sprig to garnish

50 g (¼ cup) smoked salmon trimmings, roughly chopped

1 teaspoon olive oil

1 tablespoon freshly grated Parmesan

salt and freshly ground black pepper

METHOD

1 In a large bowl, mix together the egg yolks, garlic and tarragon, and season. Stir in the smoked salmon.

2 In a separate bowl, whisk the egg whites until they form soft peaks, then fold into the egg yolk mixture.

3 Heat the olive oil in a 20 cm (8 in) non-stick frying-pan and pour in the egg mixture. Cook gently over a low to medium heat for 2–3 minutes until golden brown underneath. You can check how brown the omelette is by gently lifting the edge with a knife.

4 Pre-heat the grill to medium. Sprinkle the Parmesan over the omelette and pop under the grill for 3–4 minutes until golden and set. Slide on to a plate and serve.

CHEF'S TIP: Pile arugula or watercress into the center of the omelette and sprinkle with balsamic or olive oil for a great tasting variation.

Creamy salmon spaghetti

It's amazing how such a simple dish can turn out so stylishly. I've chosen to use the tail fillet of salmon as it's thinner than the thick fillets from the middle of the fish, which means it'll cook more quickly and it's more economical, too. I know I always say don't add Parmesan to fishy pasta, but in this case, believe me, it's delicious.

PREPARATION: 5 minutes COOKING TIME: 15 minutes

SERVES 4

300 g (11 oz) spaghetti

300 ml carton heavy cream

2 garlic cloves

2 teaspoons tomato paste

250 g (9 oz) skinless, boneless salmon tail fillet

4 tablespoons freshly grated Parmesan, plus extra, to serve

salt and freshly ground black pepper

METHOD

1 Cook the pasta in a large pan of boiling, salted water according to the packet instructions.

2 Meanwhile, pour the cream into a small pan and crush in the garlic cloves. Stir in the tomato paste and heat gently. Cut the fish widthways into 1cm (½ inch) wide strips and, once the cream is hot, stir in the salmon and remove from the heat (the heat from the cream will cook the fish in about 3–4 minutes). Add salt and pepper to taste.

3 Drain the pasta and return to the pan. Stir in the salmon mixture and the Parmesan, then divide between bowls. Pass round more Parmesan for sprinkling over.

Tuna and parsley tagliatelle

This is one of those dishes that I can always knock up when I haven't had time to get in the shopping – it's a real store-cupboard savior and it's very tasty too. Like most fishy pasta dishes, hold the Parmesan.

PREPARATION: 10 minutes COOKING TIME: 15 minutes

SERVES 2

200 g (1 cup) dried tagliatelle

3 tablespoons olive oil

1 small onion, finely chopped

2 garlic cloves, finely chopped

1 red chili, seeded and finely chopped

250 g (1 cup) chestnut mushrooms, halved

1 can tuna in spring water or brine, drained

4 tablespoons chopped fresh parsley

salt and freshly ground black pepper

METHOD

1 Cook the pasta in a large pan of boiling salted water, according to the packet instructions.

2 Meanwhile, heat 2 tablespoons of the oil in a large frying-pan and cook the onion, garlic and chili for 2–3 minutes. Add the mushrooms and cook for a further 3–4 minutes until beginning to brown. Stir in the tuna and 2–3 tablespoons of boiling water from the pasta pan. Add salt and pepper to taste.

3 Drain the pasta well and return to the pan. Stir in the tuna mixture, the parsley and remaining tablespoon of olive oil. Divide between 2 bowls and serve topped with a good grinding of black pepper.

CHEF'S TIP: My wife likes a dollop of crème fraîche on top of her pasta, and I have to say it really does taste good.

Fresh charred tuna steak
with salsa verde

Oh, I love a bit of salsa verde. It translates simply as 'green sauce', and I vary it frequently to include my favorite flavorings (or whatever's in my store-cupboard). This version is fantastic with most plain grilled or fried fish and is a perfect match for a fresh tuna steak. I like it quite rough, so I prefer to chop it by hand, but you can give it a quick blitz in the blender if you prefer.

PREPARATION: 15 minutes COOKING TIME: 10 minutes

SERVES 4

2 anchovy fillets

1 tablespoon salted capers

1 green chili, seeded and finely chopped

1 garlic clove, crushed

3 tablespoons chopped fresh parsley

1 tablespoon chopped fresh coriander

2 teaspoons Dijon mustard

4 tablespoons olive oil

1 tablespoon white wine vinegar

4 x 150–200 g (5–7 oz) tuna steaks

salt and freshly ground black pepper

METHOD

1 Place the anchovy fillets and capers on to a large board and, using a heavy knife, finely chop them. Place the chili and garlic on top and chop again until finely minced.

2 Scrape into a bowl and stir in the herbs, mustard, 3 tablespoons of the oil and the vinegar. Season with black pepper and set aside.

3 Pre-heat a ridged grill pan or heavy, non-stick frying-pan. Lightly brush the tuna with oil and season with salt and pepper. Cook for 3–4 minutes on each side until just cooked through but still a little pink in the center. Transfer to 4 serving plates and spoon over the salsa. Serve immediately.

Fresh charred tuna steak with salsa verde *with* Fennel, orange and olive salad (page 132)

French-style roasted cod

This is a beautifully easy, rustic-style dish, packed with flavor. Serve at the table so your guests see it, still sizzling, in its roasting pan.

PREPARATION: 15 minutes COOKING TIME: 25 minutes

SERVES 4

450 g (1 lb) potatoes such as Maris Piper, peeled and cubed

1 garlic bulb

4 plum tomatoes

4 rosemary sprigs

3 tablespoons olive oil

4 x 150 g (5 oz) thick boneless cod fillets, skin on

4 tablespoons white wine

salt and freshly ground black pepper

handful of fresh basil leaves, to garnish

METHOD

1 Pre-heat the oven to 220°C/425°F/Gas 7. Cook the potatoes in a large pan of boiling water for 10 minutes until almost tender and starting to crumble slightly around the edges.

2 Drain the potatoes well and transfer to a large roasting pan. Break the garlic bulb and nestle the cloves between the potatoes. Roughly chop the tomatoes and sprinkle with the rosemary. Season generously, then drizzle over 2 tablespoons of the olive oil. Roast for 15 minutes.

3 Add the cod fillets to the pan, allowing them to rest on top of the potatoes and tomatoes. Drizzle the remaining oil over the top, season the fish and cook for 5 minutes. Splash in the wine and cook for a further 5 minutes until the fish is just cooked.

4 Tear over the basil leaves and serve straight from the pan. Remember to remind your guests that they'll need to peel the cloves of garlic before they eat them.

French-style roasted cod

Oven-baked
mussel and cherry tomato risotto

This is a delightful supper dish. The combination of fresh mussels and a delicious, moist wine and herb-scented tomato risotto is perfect. You'll need to get hold of a large roasting pan and some strong, wide kitchen foil before you start.

PREPARATION: 15 minutes COOKING TIME: 45 minutes

SERVES 4

350 g (12 oz) cherry tomatoes

1 red onion, finely chopped

1 tablespoon olive oil

300 g (1½ cups) risotto rice such as Arborio or Carnaroli

150 ml (½ cup) white wine

750 ml (2½ cups) hot vegetable stock

2 sprigs fresh rosemary

1 kg (2¼ lb) small, live mussels, cleaned

2 tablespoons chopped fresh parsley

salt and freshly ground black pepper

METHOD

1 Pre-heat the oven to 200°C/400°F/Gas 6. Place the cherry tomatoes in a large roasting ann and sprinkle with the red onion. Drizzle with olive oil and salt and pepper and roast for 10 minutes.

2 Add the rice, wine, stock, rosemary and some salt and pepper and return to the oven for 20 minutes until the rice is almost tender and the liquid has almost all been absorbed. Scatter the mussels over the top of the rice. Cover tightly with foil and return to the oven for 15 minutes.

3 Remove the roasting tin from the oven, lift the foil and check the mussels, discarding any that haven't opened. Sprinkle with the chopped parsley. Serve at the table immediately, allowing guests to help themselves.

Oven-baked mussel and cherry tomato risotto

Tandoori-tikka king shrimp

This isn't a classic Indian dish, it's one that I've brought together in the style of my favorite tandoori and tikka dry-cooked dishes. Serve it with a dollop of raita (or even tzatsiki) and a pile of chapatis, which you can now buy in supermarkets.

PREPARATION: 10 minutes COOKING TIME: 5 minutes

SERVES 4

1 garlic clove, crushed

1 teaspoon ground cumin

½ teaspoon chili powder

½ teaspoon ground turmeric

½ teaspoon salt

¾ cup natural yogurt

few drops of red food coloring (optional)

20 large raw, tiger shrimp, shelled but tail section left intact

1 lemon, cut into wedges, chapatis and raita, to serve

METHOD

1 In a large, shallow dish, mix together the garlic, cumin, chilli, turmeric, salt, yogurt and food coloring. Add the shrimp and stir well to coat.

2 Pre-heat the grill to high, or heat a large, non-stick frying pan. Thread the shrimp on to soaked bamboo skewers and cook for 5 minutes, turning until the coating is dark red and the shrimp are cooked through. Serve with lemon wedges, raita and chapatis.

CHEF'S TIP: To make a quick raita, mix together a carton of natural yogurt with some grated or diced cucumber, a crushed garlic clove, pinch of salt and sugar and some chopped fresh mint.

Tandoori-tikka king shrimp

Crispy lemon fusion chicken

This may seem rather strange at first, cooking the floured chicken without any added fat, but providing you cook it good and slowly, the skin will gradually release enough fat to prevent any burning. The wine and stock are nicely thickened up by the cornstarch, making a delicious France-meets-China fusion dish that you could serve French-style with puréed potatoes and green beans, or Chinese-style with boiled rice, bok choy and a splash of soy sauce.

PREPARATION: 15 minutes COOKING TIME: 30 minutes

SERVES 4

2 garlic cloves, finely chopped

grated rind and juice of 1 lemon

2 teaspoons Dijon mustard

1 teaspoon fresh thyme leaves plus 4 sprigs

8 boneless chicken thighs with skin on

3 tablespoons cornstarch

100 ml (½ cup) white wine

100 ml (½ cup) chicken stock

salt and freshly ground black pepper

METHOD

1 Mix together the garlic, lemon rind, mustard, thyme leaves and some salt and pepper. Season the chicken thighs, then pull the skin back from the flesh. Spread with the mustard mixture, then stretch the skin back into place.

2 Season the cornstarch with salt and pepper then roll the chicken thighs in the mixture. Set a large non-stick frying-pan over a low heat and, when hot, add the chicken thighs, skin-side down. Cook for 20 minutes without turning until the skin is crunchy and deep golden and the chicken is almost completely cooked through.

3 Turn over the chicken, pouring off any excess fat. Pour in the wine and lemon juice and add the thyme sprigs, then raise the heat and bubble rapidly for 3–4 minutes. Add the stock and simmer for a further 2–3 minutes until the sauce is smooth and thickened and the chicken is cooked through. Serve warm.

Oriental steamed
soy chicken and vegetables

For a really delicious low-fat meal that's healthy and easy to make, make a date with my Oriental Steamed Soy Chicken – you'll be hooked. To make this recipe you will need a large, two-tiered Oriental bamboo steamer.

PREPARATION: 10 minutes COOKING TIME: 15 minutes

SERVES 2

4 tablespoon soy sauce

1 tablespoon honey

pinch chili flakes

2 chicken breasts or 4 chicken thighs, skinned, boned and cut into strips

100 g (½ cup) choi sum or bok choy

75 g (⅓ cup) shiitake mushrooms

50 g (2 oz) bean sprouts

2 green onions, thinly sliced

boiled rice, to serve

METHOD

1   Mix the soy sauce, honey and chili together in a shallow bowl. Add the chicken pieces, then place in a bamboo steamer. Cover and sit over a pan of boiling water for 10 minutes.

2   Cut the choi sum into 12 cm (4¾ inch) lengths or quarter the bok choy, and halve the mushrooms. Toss together and place in a second layer of the bamboo steamer. Scatter the bean sprouts and green onions over the top.

3   Lift the steamer containing the chicken off the top of the pan and sit the vegetable tier underneath – it is crucial that the vegetables sit beneath the chicken otherwise the juices they release will all fall into the bowl holding the chicken and dilute the soy dressing.

4   Return the bamboo stack to the pan and continue to steam for a further 3–4 minutes until the vegetables are tender but still crisp and the chicken is cooked through.

5   Serve the bamboo steamer stack at the table with the rice, and allow guests to help themselves.

Mediterranean chicken caesar
with aïoli and foccacia croutons

This dish takes you on a Mediterranean tour with Italian croutons, Spanish dressing and Greek-style marinated chicken. Eat it in your back garden on a sunny afternoon and it'll be easy to imagine yourself in a Provençal olive grove.

PREPARATION: 20 minutes + marinating time COOKING TIME: 20 minutes

SERVES 4

4 skinless, boneless chicken breasts

1 tablespoon chopped fresh rosemary

1 teaspoon dried oregano

1 shallot, finely chopped

100 ml (½ cup) red or white wine

2 tablespoons olive oil

salt and freshly ground black pepper

1 romaine lettuce

FOR THE AÏOLI

4 tablespoons mayonnaise

1 crushed garlic clove

squeeze of fresh lemon juice

FOR THE CROUTONS

2 mini foccacia, or half a medium loaf, about 150 g (5 oz)

1 tablespoon olive oil

2 tablespoons freshly grated Parmesan

METHOD

1 Place the chicken breasts, rosemary, oregano, shallot, wine and olive oil in a shallow dish. Season with salt and pepper and set aside to marinate for at least 1 hour, but preferably overnight. Meanwhile, for the aïoli, mix the mayonnaise with the garlic then squeeze in a little lemon juice to taste.

2 Pre-heat the oven to 200°C/400°F/Gas 6. Remove the chicken from the marinade and place on a baking sheet. Roast for 20 minutes until golden brown and cooked through.

3 Meanwhile, make the croutons: cut the foccacia into cubes and toss with the olive oil and Parmesan. Scatter on to a baking sheet, ensuring they are in a single layer. Bake with the chicken for 5–10 minutes until crisp and golden brown, then remove from the oven and allow to cool.

4 Remove the chicken from the oven and allow to cool slightly, then cut diagonally into strips. Tear the romaine lettuce into bite-sized pieces and place in a large salad bowl. Toss with the chicken strips, aïoli and croutons and serve while the chicken is still warm.

Mediterranean chicken caesar with aïoli and foccacia croutons

Chicken, sage and Cheddar
en croûte

Delicious straight from the oven or cooled and packed into a lunch box or picnic basket with a simple green salad. If you are serving these hot, try pairing them with my fiery Cracked Tapas Patatas Bravas on page 124.

PREPARATION: 15 minutes COOKING TIME: 25 minutes

SERVES 4

375 g pack ready-rolled puff pastry

4 small, skinless, boneless chicken breasts, each about 75 g (3 oz)

1 tablespoon Dijon mustard

8 fresh sage leaves

150 g (1¼ cups) coarsely grated Cheddar

1 tablespoon milk

salt and freshly ground black pepper

METHOD

1 Pre-heat the oven to 200°C/400°F/Gas 6. Open out the pastry on to a lightly floured board and roll out slightly so it is large enough to cut into four 15 x 20 cm (6 x 8 inch) rectangles. Spread the center of each rectangle with the mustard and place a chicken fillet on each. Season with salt and pepper then place 2 sage leaves on each fillet.

2 Scatter the cheese evenly over each fillet, then dampen the edges of the pastry with a little water. Fold the pastry over to enclose the filling, squeezing together the edges between finger and thumb to ensure no melted cheese can escape during baking.

3 Transfer the parcels to a baking sheet, seam side down, then brush each with a little milk. Bake for 25 minutes until the pastry is crisp and deep golden and the chicken has cooked through. Serve hot or cold.

CHEF'S TIP: If you want to decorate your parcels, use a small, sharp knife to score a sage-shaped leaf on top of each before brushing with milk and baking. Alternatively, if you have any pastry trimmings left over, re-roll them, cut out leaf shapes and stick one to the surface of each parcel with a little water before baking.

Madras coconut, chicken
and banana curry

Moist, tender pieces of chicken in a rich almond, coconut and banana sauce –
always a dinner winner in my house.

PREPARATION: 15 minutes COOKING TIME: 30 minutes

SERVES 4

1 teaspoon garam masala

1 tablespoon vegetable oil

8 skinless, boneless chicken thighs, halved

1 large onion, thinly sliced

2 tomatoes, roughly chopped

450 ml (2 cups) chicken stock

2 tablespoons hot curry paste

142 ml carton heavy cream

50 g (¼ cup) ground almonds

25 g (2 tablespoons) desiccated coconut

2 large bananas

boiled rice, to serve

2 tablespoons roughly chopped fresh coriander

1 lemon cut into wedges, to garnish

METHOD

1 Mix together the chicken pieces, garam masala and some salt and
pepper. Heat the oil in a large pan and add the chicken and onion and cook
for 10 minutes, stirring occasionally until golden brown.

2 Add the tomatoes and cook for 2 minutes until beginning to soften.
Pour in the stock, stir in the curry paste, then bring to the boil and simmer
for 10 minutes.

3 Stir in the cream, almonds and the coconut. Peel the bananas and cut
into 2 cm (¾ inch) thick slices. Add to the pan, season with salt and pepper
to taste and simmer for 5 minutes until the bananas are just tender.

4 Divide between 4 plates and serve each with boiled rice, a sprinkling of
fresh coriander and a wedge of lemon for squeezing over.

Coriander and lime chicken

I'm always looking for new ways of serving chicken, especially ones that are quick to make and really tasty. This dish is a real winner. I like to serve it with jasmine rice, steamed greens and a spicy dipping sauce (see Crispy Noodle-wrapped Shrimp with Rice-wine Dipping Sauce, page 34). Leftovers are great served up the next day with a salad or in a French-bread sandwich.

PREPARATION: 15 minutes + marinating time COOKING TIME: 15 minutes

SERVES 4

6 garlic cloves

4 tablespoons fresh coriander leaves, plus extra, to garnish

2 teaspoons black peppercorns, coarsely ground

2 teaspoons fine granulated sugar

juice of 2 limes

2 teaspoons Thai fish sauce (nam pla)

1 tablespoon light soy sauce

1 tablespoon sunflower oil

4 skinless, boneless chicken breasts

METHOD

1 Finely chop the garlic and coriander then mix in the peppercorns, sugar, lime juice, fish sauce, soy sauce and sunflower oil until well blended. Place the chicken breasts in the marinade and set aside for 1–2 hours, turning from time to time.

2 Pre-heat a ridged grill or heavy, non-stick frying-pan and cook the chicken for 7–8 minutes on each side until the chicken is cooked through and golden brown with good bar-marks. Serve hot or cold, garnished with coriander leaves.

CHEF'S TIP: The marinade contains lime juice, which tenderizes the chicken. After more than a few hours though, the meat fibres can become so soft that the chicken literally falls apart, which means that this dish is not suitable for overnight marinating.

Coriander and lime chicken *with* Simple wok noodles (page 133)

Superb lemon herb chicken
with roast potatoes

I know everyone thinks they know how to roast a chicken, but as this is the best recipe for a roast chicken in the whole world, I thought I'd share it with you. I have a chicken brick that I often cook this in, as it comes out moist and juicy with a miraculously crisp skin. If you don't own one (they cost around £10 from cook shops), cook it in the oven as detailed here. And don't save roast chicken and potatoes for Sundays, it's ideal for a casual after-work dinner party.

PREPARATION: 20 minutes COOKING TIME: 1½ hours

SERVES 4

1 medium chicken, about 1.5 kg (3¼ lb)

1 large lemon

large sprig of sage

large sprig of rosemary

25 g (2 tablespoons) butter, at room temperature

2 garlic cloves, crushed

1 tablespoon olive oil

750 g (1½ lb) floury potatoes, such as King Edward or Maris Piper

sea salt and freshly ground black pepper

METHOD

1 Pre-heat the oven to 200°C/400°F/Gas 6. Snip any strings that are binding the chicken legs, then wipe inside the cavity with paper towel and season. Cut the lemon into 5 or 6 pieces and push them into the cavity with the sage and rosemary sprigs.

2 Mix together the butter and garlic with some salt and pepper. Loosen the skin on the breast then, using your fingers, spread the butter between the flesh and the skin. Pull the skin back into place. Place the bird in a large roasting pan and brush all over with a little oil and a sprinkling of coarse salt. Roast for 30 minutes.

3 Meanwhile, peel and cube the potatoes then cook in a pan of boiling water for exactly 5 minutes. Drain in a colander then shake vigorously to 'fluff up' the outside of the potatoes – this helps give them a lovely, crunchy finish when they are roasted.

4 Open the oven and quickly toss the potatoes into the pan, shaking to coat them in the buttery chicken juices. Return to the oven for 1 hour, without turning or poking until the chicken is cooked through and golden and the potatoes are crunchy and golden on the outside and fluffy and floury on the inside. Cut the chicken into quarters and serve with the pan juices and roasties.

Superb lemon herb chicken with roast potatoes

Jamaican jerk chicken

I like to use chicken on the bone for my jerk chicken and find if I ask the butcher to cut a whole chicken into quarters, everyone gets to choose the piece they like best. Me, I'm a breast man.

PREPARATION: 20 minutes + marinating time COOKING TIME: 45 minutes

SERVES 4

2 onions, about 200 g (7 oz), roughly chopped

2 Scotch bonnet chilies, seeded and roughly chopped

2 garlic cloves

4 cm (1½ inch) piece ginger root, roughly chopped

2 teaspoons fresh marjoram leaves or fresh thyme

½ teaspoon ground allspice

120 ml (½ cup) cider vinegar

120 ml (½ cup) soy sauce

1 tablespoon honey

1.5 kg (3¼ lb) chicken (medium), quartered or 4 chicken quarters

salt and freshly ground black pepper

METHOD

1 Place the onions, chilies, garlic, ginger and marjoram in a food processor and blitz until well blended. Add the allspice, cider vinegar, soy sauce and honey and whizz again until smooth. Add salt and pepper to taste.

2 Deeply slash the chicken then place in a large, shallow dish. Pour over the sauce and chill for 2–3 hours, or overnight.

3 Pre-heat the oven to 200°C/400°F/Gas 6. Transfer the chicken to a rack and sit it inside a roasting pan. Pour over the marinade and roast for 40–45 minutes, basting occasionally with the marinating juices in the roasting pan until cooked through and blackened.

CHEF'S TIP: Jerk Chicken is delicious served with Peppy's Rice and Peas (see page 123).

This dish is also great cooked over medium-hot coals on the barbecue for 25–30 minutes. You'll need to baste it with the marinade and turn it occasionally to make sure it is thoroughly cooked.

Tender turkey and peanut butter curry

Normally seen at Christmas or Thanksgiving, turkey is an amazingly versatile, healthy and good-value food and deserves to be eaten all-year round. Here's a quick, one-pot recipe to whet your appetite.

PREPARATION: 15 minutes COOKING TIME: 45 minutes

SERVES 4

2 tablespoons vegetable oil

500 g (1 lb 2 oz) turkey medallions or breast fillets, cubed

1 onion, chopped

2 garlic cloves, chopped

2 green chilies, seeded and chopped

2 teaspoons chopped fresh ginger

2 tablespoons Madras curry powder

400 g can chopped tomatoes

200 ml carton coconut cream

2 tablespoons crunchy peanut butter

2 tablespoons chopped fresh coriander

salt and freshly ground black pepper

pilau rice, to serve

METHOD

1 Pre-heat the oven to 190°C/375°F/Gas 5. Heat the oil in a casserole dish and stir-fry the turkey, onion, garlic, chilies, ginger and curry powder for 5 minutes until beginning to brown.

2 Add some salt and pepper then stir in the tomatoes, coconut cream and peanut butter. Cover with a tightly fitting lid and bake for 45 minutes. Check the seasoning, stir in the coriander and serve with pilau rice.

Cinnamon-scented duck
on cherry sauce

Call me old-fashioned if you like, but this is a classic and I want to see it back on our tables. You don't need to add any oil to the pan when frying the duck as the natural fat will be released as it cooks. Serve with Rösti Dauphinoise (page 122).

PREPARATION: 15 minutes + 1 hour marinating time   COOKING TIME: 15 minutes

SERVES 4

4 x 225 g (8 oz) skin-on duck breasts

½ teaspoon sea salt

½ teaspoon ground cinnamon

100 ml (½ cup) ruby port

425 g can pitted black cherries in syrup

4 fresh thyme sprigs, plus extra for garnish, if desired

½ teaspoon balsamic vinegar

METHOD

1 Prick the skin on the duck breasts with a fork, then rub in the salt and cinnamon. Place the port, the juice from the cherries and the thyme in a shallow dish and sit the duck skin-side up in the mixture so the flesh marinates while the skin takes in the salt and cinnamon. Set aside for 1 hour.

2 Pat the duck dry. Heat a large, non-stick frying-pan and cook the duck, skin-side down for 8–10 minutes until crisp and golden. Remove the duck from the pan and drain off all the excess fat.

3 Return the duck to the pan skin-side up. Pour round the marinade mixture, bring to the boil and simmer for 12–15 minutes until the duck is cooked through but still a little pink in the center. Remove the duck from the pan and rest on a plate for a few minutes.

4 Check the seasoning and stir in the cherries and balsamic vinegar. Simmer for a minute or two until the cherries are warmed through. Then, spoon the cherry sauce onto the plates, place the breasts on top of the sauce and garnish with a sprig of fresh thyme, if desired.

Cinnamon-scented duck on cherry sauce *with* Rösti dauphinoise (page 122)

Warm Oriental duck
and mango salad

It's essential that food looks good as well as tasting terrific – and this salad looks and tastes fabulous. It's also low in fat and quick to prepare – the perfect Oriental nosh.

PREPARATION: 15 minutes COOKING TIME: 5 minutes

SERVES 4

450 g (1 lb) skinless, boneless duck breasts

1 teaspoon Chinese five spice

1 teaspoon sunflower oil

FOR THE DRESSING

juice of 1 lime

1 teaspoon Thai fish sauce (nam pla)

1 tablespoon soy sauce

2 teaspoons clear honey

FOR THE SALAD

80 g bag mixed greens

1 small mango, skinned, stoned and cut into matchsticks

100 g (¾ cup) bean sprouts

4 green onions, shredded

fresh mint leaves and toasted sesame seeds, to garnish

METHOD

1 Cut the duck into 1 cm (¾ inch) wide strips and mix with the five spice. Heat the oil in a wok or large frying-pan and, when hot, add the duck strips and stir-fry for exactly 2 minutes until nicely browned but still a little pink in the center.

2 Transfer to a large bowl and stir in the lime juice, fish sauce, soy sauce and clear honey. Set aside to cool to room temperature.

3 To serve, place the salad leaves in a large serving bowl and toss with the mango, bean sprouts and duck with dressing. Sprinkle with the shredded green onions, mint and sesame seeds and serve.

CHEF'S TIP: This is a very pretty dish, but for added attraction, place the shredded green onions in a bowl of iced water so they curl.

Lasagna
with smoked ham and minted peas

This is one of those great pasta recipes that are ready to serve in the time it takes the pasta to cook. If you fancy it, stir in a slosh of double cream just before serving.

PREPARATION: 5 minutes COOKING TIME: 10 minutes

SERVES 4

300 g (11 oz) dried lasagna or other pasta ribbons

2 tablespoons olive oil

1 small onion, finely chopped

200 g (7 oz) thick-cut smoked ham

150 g (1¼ cups) frozen peas, thawed

splash of white wine, stock or water, about 4 tablespoons

2 tablespoons chopped fresh mint

salt and freshly ground black pepper

freshly grated Parmesan, to serve

METHOD

1   Cook the pasta in a large pan of boiling, salted water, according to the package instructions.

2   Meanwhile, heat the oil in a frying-pan and cook the onion for 3–4 minutes until beginning to soften.

3   Cut the smoked ham into strips about 5 mm (¼ inch) wide and 3 cm (1¼ inches) long. Add to the pan and cook for 1 minute then add the peas and liquid and simmer for 4–5 minutes until the liquid has evaporated. Season to taste with a little salt and plenty of black pepper.

4   Drain the pasta and return to the pan. Add the pea mixture and the mint and toss well together. Divide between bowls and pass round the Parmesan.

Crusted roast sirloin
with crispy speckled onion rings

This is my ideal Saturday supper – roasted rsirloin with a caper, tomato and basil crust, lots of crispy onion rings – and it takes minimum time to prepare. Serve with a robust red wine and a crisp green salad.

PREPARATION: 20 minutes COOKING TIME: 25 minutes

SERVES 4

1 Spanish onion

300 ml (1 cup) milk

vegetable oil, for frying

6 tablespoons self-rising flour

2 teaspoons snipped chives

salt and freshly ground black pepper

FOR THE STEAKS

4 x 150 g (5 oz) steaks

1 slice of white bread, about 50 g (2 oz)

12 capers

4 sun-dried tomatoes in oil, roughly chopped

1 ripe tomato, roughly chopped

1 tablespoon of olive oil, or oil from the sun-dried tomato jar

handful of fresh basil, roughly chopped

METHOD

1 Begin by putting the onion rings in to soak for a minimum of 15 minutes. Cut the onion into 1 cm (½ inch) wide slices and separate the rings. Pour over the milk and set aside, turning the onion rings occasionally. Take the steaks out of the fridge and leave at room temperature for 20 minutes or so.

2 Pre-heat the oven to 220°C/425°F/Gas 7. Break the bread into pieces and whizz in a food processor to form rough crumbs. Remove and set aside. Then, place the capers, sun-dried and fresh tomatoes, the oil, basil and some salt and pepper in the food processor and whizz until pulped. Add the breadcrumbs and pulse once more until evenly mixed.

3 Place the steaks on a lightly oiled baking sheet and spoon over the tomato-crumb mixture. Cook in the oven for 10 minutes until the steaks are browned but still a little pink in the center. Meanwhile, heat 5 cm (2 inches) of oil in a deep frying pan. Mix together the flour, chives and some salt and pepper. Drain the onion rings, dust in the flour, shaking off any excess, then fry in batches for 2–3 minutes until crisp and golden brown. Drain on kitchen paper.

4 Transfer the steaks to 4 warm serving plates and allow to rest for a few minutes. Pile the speckled onion rings on the side, garnish with fresh basil leaves and serve.

Crusted roast sirloin with crispy speckled onion rings

One-pot chunky
beef bourguignonne

This is a classic that never fails to go down well. And while you've got the oven on, why not pop in some Rösti Dauphinoise (page 122). It's an ideal accompaniment, as is my scrumptious Soft, Bellissima Dolcelatte Polenta (page 118). Ooh, so exciting, and all in one pot, too.

PREPARATION: 20 minutes COOKING TIME: 2 hours

SERVES 6

2 tablespoons olive oil

750 g (1½ lb) cubed braising or stewing steak

3 tablespoons flour, seasoned with salt and pepper

9 shallots, halved

3 garlic cloves, halved

125 g (4½ oz) lardons or cubed pancetta

750 ml bottle red wine

2 sprigs fresh thyme

1 tablespoon tomato paste

1 cup button mushrooms

salt and freshly ground black pepper

METHOD

1 Pre-heat the oven to 180°C/350°F/Gas 4. Set a 3 litre (5½ pint) flameproof casserole with a lid over the heat and add the olive oil.

2 Toss the meat in the seasoned flour then cook in batches in the hot oil for 3–4 minutes until nicely browned. Remove each batch with a slotted spoon and set aside. Now cook the shallots, garlic and pancetta in the pan for 5 minutes, stirring frequently until golden brown.

3 Return the meat to the pan then pour in the wine and bring to a steaming boil. Stir in the thyme, tomato paste and some seasoning. Cover with the lid and cook in the oven for 1 hour. Add the mushrooms, cover and return to the oven for a further 30–45 minutes until the meat is tender. Serve straight from the casserole.

One-pot chunky beef bourguignonne *with* Soft, bellissima, Dolcelatte polenta (page 118)

Spicy Thai beef salad

A delicious, hot, sweet-and-sour salad which is typical of north-east Thailand. It also traditionally includes some ground rice, which I like, but can be skipped if you're short on time. I serve it with some sticky Thai rice for a lovely supper or dinner-party main course.

PREPARATION: 25 minutes COOKING TIME: 1 minute

SERVES 4

4 tablespoons long-grain rice

juice of 2 limes

4 tablespoons Thai fish sauce (nam pla)

1 tablespoon fine granulated sugar

½ teaspoon chilli powder

2 shallots, very thinly sliced

2 garlic cloves, finely chopped

2 tablespoons chopped fresh mint leaves

1 Thai red chilli, thinly sliced

1 tablespoon vegetable oil

450 g (1 lb) tender steak, such as sirloin or fillet, cut into fine 1 x 3 cm (½ x 1¼ inch) strips

FOR THE SALAD

1 heart of romaine lettuce, roughly torn

1 cup bean sprouts

1 cup fine green beans, blanched and cooled

METHOD

1 Heat a large, non-stick frying pan and cook the rice for a couple of minutes, stirring until the grains start to turn golden and begin to pop. Transfer to a pestle and mortar and grind to a coarse powder.

2 Arrange the salad on 4 serving plates.

3 In a large bowl, stir together the lime juice, fish sauce, sugar and chili powder, mixing until well blended. Stir in the shallots, garlic, mint, fresh chili and ground rice.

4 Heat the oil in the pan and, when very hot, add the beef and stir-fry for exactly 30 seconds until browned on the outside but still pink in the center. Stir into the dressing bowl then, while still slightly warm, spoon over the salad. Serve immediately.

CHEF'S TIP: This can be made in advance; just stir-fry the steak at the last minute and spoon over the salad.

Spicy Thai beef salad

Lamb, mint and chili strudels

This is the most brilliant way to use left-over lamb. I tend to shred whatever's left of the Sunday roast of lamb and turn it into these delicious strudels which, when paired with a salad such as my Fennel, Orange and Olive Salad (page 132) make a lovely, light supper. Like my Chicken, Sage and Cheddar en Croûte (page 68), these are perfect for picnics or packed lunches.

PREPARATION: 15 minutes COOKING TIME: 15 minutes

SERVES 4

300 g (11 oz) cooked lamb, shredded

2 tablespoons mint jelly

1 teaspoon West Indian hot pepper sauce or good dash of Tabasco

salt and freshly ground black pepper

4 sheets filo pastry

spoonful of butter, melted

METHOD

1 Pre-heat the oven to 220°C/425°F/Gas 7. Mix together the lamb, mint jelly and pepper sauce. Add salt and pepper to taste.

2 Open out a sheet of filo pastry and top with one quarter of the mixture. Fold 1 cm (½ inch) of the edges on the longer side of the pastry over the filling, then roll up like a swiss roll. Arrange seam side down on a non-stick baking sheet.

3 Repeat to make 4 rolls. Brush with melted butter and bake for 12–15 minutes until crisp and golden brown.

Lightning lamb cassoulet

A classic French cassoulet takes ages to prepare and cook. My simplified version is tasty, easy and pretty quick to get together. It's hearty, so make sure your guests are good and hungry.

PREPARATION: 10 minutes COOKING TIME: 1 hour 15 minutes

SERVES 4

1 tablespoon olive oil

8 lamb cutlets

1 small onion, finely chopped

2 garlic cloves, finely chopped

2 cups chopped tomatoes

1 teaspoon dried herbes de Provence

1 teaspoon brown sugar

1 tablespoon red wine vinegar

150 ml (½ cup) lamb stock

2 x 400 g can cannellini beans, drained

75 g (1¼ cups) fresh white breadcrumbs

salt and freshly ground white pepper

METHOD

1 Pre-heat the oven to 180°C/350°F/Gas 4. Heat the oil in a large frying-pan and quickly brown the lamb cutlets for 2 minutes on each side. Remove from the pan and transfer to a 2 litre (3½ pint) casserole dish.

2 Add the onion and garlic to the pan and cook for 3–4 minutes until softened and golden. Add the tomatoes, herbs, sugar, vinegar and lamb stock and simmer together for 2–3 minutes. Add salt and pepper to taste.

3 Empty the beans over the lamb cutlets then roughly stir in the tomato mixture. Sprinkle the breadcrumbs on top of the casserole in an even layer, cover and bake for 30 minutes. Remove the cover and cook for a further 30 minutes until bubbling and golden brown on top.

Lamb shank Rogan Josh

Rogan Josh is one of those classic Indian dishes which has many interpretations. This is my version and it's lovely. I like to use meat on the bone such as lamb shanks, as the bones add flavor to the dish while the lamb slow-cooks until meltingly tender. Pair it with my Easy Pilau Rice (page 128) for a delicious supper.

PREPARATION: 25 minutes COOKING TIME: 2½–3 hours

SERVES 4

2 tablespoons all-purpose flour

1 tablespoon chili powder

1 teaspoon ground coriander

½ teaspoon ground ginger

½ teaspoon salt

pinch of nutmeg

4 lamb shanks, each about 500 g (1 lb 2 oz)

2 tablespoons vegetable oil

1 large onion, thinly sliced

300 ml (1¼ cups) Greek-style natural yogurt

450 ml (1½ cups) hot lamb stock

4 cardamom pods, cracked

1 pinch saffron strands

4 small tomatoes, each cut into 6 wedges

METHOD

1 Mix together the flour, chili powder, coriander, ginger, salt and nutmeg. Dust the lamb shanks in the flour, reserving any excess.

2 Pre-heat the oven to 180°C/350°F/Gas 4. Pour the oil into a large roasting pan and place over a high heat. Cook the lamb shanks for 10 minutes, turning until well browned, then transfer to a large plate and set aside.

3 Add the onion to the pan and cook for 10 minutes until golden brown. Add the reserved spiced flour and cook for 1 minute, stirring continuously. Stir in the yogurt and stock.

4 Return the lamb to the pan. Add the cardamom and saffron and bring to the boil. Cover tightly with foil and cook for 1½ hours. Add the tomato wedges and cook for a further 40–60 minutes until the lamb is almost falling away from the bone. Serve hot.

CHEF'S TIP: The longer this is cooked, the more tender the lamb becomes. It can cook for up to 3 hours, but remember to keep it tightly covered and add a splash of water or stock if it starts to dry out.

Lamb shank Rogan Josh *with* Easy pilau rice (page 128) *and* Ceylonese spiced string beans (page 126)

Ainsley's special red-wine spaghetti bolognese

You all know how to make bolognese – it's a real favorite – but mine does have a great twist. I marinate it overnight in wine so it's really succulent and very tender. Go on, try it. You'll be glad you did.

PREPARATION: 20 minutes + overnight marinating COOKING TIME: 1 hour 5 minutes

SERVES 4-6

250 g (9 oz) ground beef

250 g (9 oz) ground lamb

750 ml bottle Italian red wine, such as Chianti

½ teaspoon dried oregano

1 tablespoon olive oil

1 onion, finely chopped

2 garlic cloves, finely chopped

400 g can chopped tomatoes

pinch dried chili flakes

1 tablespoon tomato paste

450 g (1 lb) dried spaghetti

3 tablespoons chopped fresh parsley

salt and freshly ground black pepper

freshly grated Parmesan, to serve

METHOD

1 Place all the ground meat in a bowl and stir in the red wine, oregano and some salt and pepper. Cover with plastic wrap and chill for at least 4 hours or up to 12.

2 Heat the oil in a large pan and cook the onion and garlic for 3–4 minutes until softened and golden. Add the meat and any wine left in the bottom of the bowl with the tomatoes, chili, tomato paste and some salt and pepper. Bring to the boil then cover and simmer for 45 minutes. Remove the lid and bubble fairly rapidly for 15 minutes until you have a rich, dark sauce.

3 Cook the spaghetti in a large pan of boiling, salted water until tender. Drain well and return to the pan.

4 Stir the parsley through the sauce and check the seasoning. Add to the pan of spaghetti and mix through. Divide between bowls and serve with freshly grated Parmesan and a few glasses of Chianti.

Ainsley's special red-wine spaghetti bolognese

Crunchy rösti-coated lamb patties

These are tasty Greek-style burgers with a difference – a crunchy potato coating that adds real bite and style to the finished dish. There is a picture of this recipe on page 125.

PREPARATION: 20 minutes COOKING TIME: 20 minutes

SERVES 4

1 shallot, roughly chopped

2 garlic cloves, roughly chopped

2 tablespoons chopped fresh mint

500 g (1 lb 2 oz) ground lamb

½ teaspoon dried rosemary

200 g (7 oz) feta, roughly chopped

2 tablespoons flour, seasoned with salt and pepper

1 large egg, beaten with 1 tablespoon cold water

1 large floury potato, such as King Edward, about 200 g (7 oz)

vegetable oil, for shallow-frying

salt and freshly ground black pepper

METHOD

1 Place the shallot, garlic and mint in the food processor and whizz until finely chopped. Add the lamb, rosemary and some salt and pepper and whizz again until the lamb is fine and well mixed. Add the feta and pulse 2–3 times until the feta is roughly mixed into the mince but isn't finely chopped.

2 Shape the mixture into 8 even-sized cakes. Dust the cakes in seasoned flour then roll in the beaten egg.

3 Coarsely grate the potato on to a large plate, then roll the patties until lightly coated in potato.

4 Heat 1 cm (½ in) of oil in a large, non-stick frying-pan and cook the patties in batches for 5 minutes on each side until crisp, golden brown and cooked through, though still a little pink in the center. Serve hot.

CHEF'S TIP: I like to serve these with a spoonful of tomato chutney or relish. And why not try them with one of the fresh tomato salsas that many supermarkets now stock?

Greek-style lamb parcels
en papillote

Succulent lamb steak cooked in onion, garlic and herbs in its own steamed parcel. Try serving with Mama's Greek Butter-bean Salad (page 112).

PREPARATION: 10 minutes COOKING TIME: 30 minutes

SERVES 4

4 x 250 g (9 oz) lamb leg steaks (bone in)

1 tablespoon olive oil

1 small red onion, thinly sliced

2 garlic cloves, finely chopped

1 teaspoon dried oregano

4 fresh bay leaves

100 ml (½ cup) white wine

1 teaspoon cracked black pepper

sea salt

METHOD

1 Pre-heat the oven to 200°C/400°F/Gas 6.

2 Cut four 40 cm (16 inch) circles out of baking parchment. Rub each circle with a little olive oil, then place a leg steak on one half. Sprinkle with the onion, garlic, oregano, and a little salt and pepper.

3 Top with a bay leaf then fold in half to form a semi-circle. Fold over the edges to seal then, just before you have completely enclosed the steak, pour in a little wine, then finish off the folding, ensuring that the steaks are completely sealed.

4 Place the parcels on a baking sheet and bake for 30 minutes. Carefully transfer each parcel to a plate and serve.

CHEF'S TIP: To make a circle out of a square of baking parchment, fold it in half along the diagonal, then fold again. Continue folding until the paper forms an arrow-head shape. Cut the opposite end to the point of the arrow into a round. When you open the paper out you should have a circle.

Braised bacon vin blanc

A nicely cured side of bacon is a wonderful thing, especially when braised in a tasty stock like this one here. I like to serve it with my Sweet-potato and Coriander Mash (page 116). Left-overs will keep, wrapped in foil in the fridge, for quite a few days and make fantastic sandwiches and salads.

PREPARATION: 10 minutes + resting time COOKING TIME: 1½ hours

SERVES 6

1 kg (2¼ lb) side of bacon

300 ml (1 cup) dry white wine

300 ml (1 cup) vegetable stock

1 teaspoon peppercorns

2 star anise

1 onion, roughly chopped

1 apple, roughly chopped

METHOD

1 Pre-heat the oven to 180°C/350°F/Gas 4. Place the bacon in a roasting tin with the wine, stock, peppercorns, star anise, onion and apple. Cover tightly with foil and roast for 1 hour.

2 Remove the foil and cook for a further 30 minutes until the bacon is golden brown. Transfer the bacon to a warm plate and let stand for at least 15 minutes before carving. Serve warm or chilled.

CHEF'S TIP: For a delicious gravy, strain the stock into a pan and thicken with a teaspoon of dissolved cornstarch. Add a tablespoonful of redcurrant jelly and a dash of balsamic vinegar, but don't add any salt.

Smoked bacon and Dolcelatte risotto

Oh, I love a good old risotto, me, and this one is special. It needs nothing more with it, except, maybe, a glass of fruity red wine.

PREPARATION: 10 minutes COOKING TIME: 30 minutes

SERVES 4

25 g (2 tablespoons) butter

1 small onion, finely chopped

1 large garlic clove, finely chopped

200 g (7 oz) bacon, cut widthways into thin strips

300 g (1½ cups) risotto rice, such as Arborio or Carnaroli

750 ml (1½ cups) hot chicken stock

2 tablespoons chopped fresh parsley

150 g (¾ cup) dolcelatte

salt and freshly ground black pepper

METHOD

1 Heat the butter in a sauté pan and cook the onion, garlic and bacon for 5 minutes until softened and golden brown. Stir in the rice and cook for 1 minute.

2 Gradually stir in the stock, cooking for about 20 minutes until the grains are tender and all the liquid has been absorbed. Stir in the parsley and season with a tiny touch of salt (the cheese you're about to add is salty) and some black pepper.

3 Roughly dice the cheese and stir into the risotto. Quickly divide the risotto between 4 bowls, before the cheese has completely melted, and finish with a good grind of black pepper.

CHEF'S TIPS: Dolcelatte is delicious in this dish but a good alternative to look out for in your local cheese shop or supermarket is creamy Gorgonzola – avoid regular Gorgonzola, often labelled as Gorgonzola picante, as its flavor is a little too strong for this recipe.

If your risotto is a little too hard by the time you come to serve it, simply stir in a little more stock and a splash of cream before you take it to the table.

Pan-fried pork chops with
glazed apples, cider and cream sauce

We all know that pork and apples go together like love and marriage, and it couldn't be proved any better than in this lovely, up to the minute classic. I like to serve it with a soft mash and some buttery greens.

PREPARATION: 10 minutes COOKING TIME: 25 minutes

SERVES 4

1 tablespoon vegetable oil

2 Cox's Orange Pippin apples, each cut into 8 wedges

4 x 200 g (7 oz) pork chops

2 sprigs fresh sage

200 ml (1 cup) dry cider

1 tablespoon redcurrant jelly

200 ml carton crème fraîche

salt and freshly ground black pepper

METHOD

1 Heat the oil in a large non-stick frying-pan and cook the apples for 3–4 minutes on each side until golden brown but still firm. Transfer to a plate and set aside.

2 Season the chops with salt and pepper and add to the pan. Cook for 5 minutes until golden brown, turning once. Add the sage and cider and simmer for 15 minutes until the chops are cooked through. Use a slotted spoon to transfer the pork to a large plate. Cover with foil and let stand for a few minutes.

3 Stir the redcurrant jelly into the pan and simmer for 2–3 minutes, stirring until the jelly dissolves. Stir in the crème fraîche and apples, heat through gently and season to taste.

4 Pour any juices from the pork into the pan, then divide the chops between 4 plates, spoon over the apples and sauce and serve with some green vegetables.

Pan-fried pork chops with glazed apples, cider and cream sauce

Herbed couscous wedges
with roast vine-tomatoes and arugula

Couscous makes a welcome change from other everyday grains such as rice. It can get a little sticky and I've used this characteristic to my advantage in this dish, where I add a little more liquid than usual and allow the couscous to set into a firm cake.

PREPARATION: 15 minutes COOKING TIME: 20 minutes

SERVES 4

pinch of saffron strands

1 crushed garlic clove

1 vegetable stock cube

300 ml (1 cup) boiling water

250 g (1¼ cups) couscous

2 tablespoons toasted pine nuts

3 tablespoons chopped fresh parsley

2 tablespoons olive oil

4 cherry tomato vines, each with 5–7 tomatoes

1 bunch arugula

1 lemon, cut into wedges

salt and freshly ground black pepper

METHOD

1 Pre-heat the oven to 200°C/400°F/Gas 6. Place the saffron, garlic and stock cube in a heatproof jug then pour over the boiling water, stirring until the cube dissolves.

2 Place the couscous in a heatproof bowl and pour over the stock mixture. Stir in the pine nuts and parsley and season to taste. Brush a 23 cm (9 inch) dinner plate with a little of the olive oil and spoon in the couscous mixture. Smooth the surface over with the back of a spoon then set aside to cool completely.

3 Place the tomatoes in a small roasting tin and drizzle with the remaining oil. Roast for 20 minutes until the tomatoes are tender and the skins have split.

4 Turn the couscous out on to a plate and cut into 4 wedges. Pile the arugula leaves on top of the couscous, then top each serving with a roasted vine of tomatoes. Drizzle over any pan juices and serve a lemon wedge on the side of each for squeezing over.

Cumin-curried chickpea
and spinach burgers

Chickpeas make a great veggie-burger base and they taste fantastic when spiced up with a little cumin seed and curry paste. If you're feeding kids, opt for a milder curry paste than the h-h-h-h-hot one I go for.

PREPARATION: 20 minutes COOKING TIME: 20 minutes

SERVES 6

1 tablespoon olive oil

1 small onion, finely chopped

2 teaspoons cumin seeds

225 g (8 oz) baby spinach

1 tablespoon hot curry paste

2 x 400 g cans chickpeas, drained

2 tablespoons crunchy peanut butter

25 g (½ cup) fresh white breadcrumbs

salt and freshly ground black pepper

vegetable oil, for shallow-frying

burger buns or salad, to serve

METHOD

1 Heat the olive oil in a large frying pan and cook the onion for 2–3 minutes until beginning to soften. Add the cumin seeds, cook for 1 minute then add the spinach and cook over a high heat for 5 minutes until the spinach has wilted and any water released has evaporated. Stir in the curry paste and remove from the heat.

2 Place the chickpeas in a food processor with the peanut butter and breadcrumbs and whizz to form a thick paste. Add the spinach mixture and some seasoning and pulse until well blended. Using damp hands, shape the mixture into 6 even-sized cakes.

3 Wipe out the frying-pan with some paper towel and heat 1–2 tablespoons of the vegetable oil. Cook the burgers in batches for 4–5 minutes on each side until golden brown. Serve warm, sandwiched in a bread bun or with a stack of fresh salad.

Clare's winter-vegetable cobbler

This is just the kind of modernized classic that's reappearing in all those trendy pub-restaurants. It's also a perfect family supper – warming, very tasty and easy to make at home.

PREPARATION: 15 minutes COOKING TIME: 50 minutes

SERVES 6

2 leeks, thickly sliced

6 small carrots, cubed

6 small parsnips, cubed

4 sage sprigs

2 tablespoons olive oil

300 ml (1 cup) vegetable stock

142 ml carton heavy cream

1 tablespoon wholegrain mustard

salt and freshly ground black pepper

FOR THE DUMPLINGS

175 g (⅞ cup) self-rising flour

½ teaspoon salt

¼ teaspoon cayenne

25 g (2 tablespoons) butter

75 g (3 oz) old Cheddar, finely grated

1 large egg

3 tablespoons milk

METHOD

1 Pre-heat the oven to 200°C/400°F/Gas 6. Place the vegetables and sage in a roasting pan, drizzle with oil and season with salt and pepper. Roast for 30 minutes until nicely browned.

2 Meanwhile, place the flour, salt, cayenne, butter and three quarters of the cheese in a food processor and whizz until well blended. Beat together the egg and 2 tablespoons of the milk then add to the food processor. Pulse to form a smooth, soft dough.

3 Mix together the stock, cream and mustard, and pour over the vegetables. Then, with floured hands, roll the dumpling mixture into 6 balls and flatten slightly with the heel of the hand. Brush the tops of the dumplings with the remaining milk, then scatter over the reserved cheese.

4 Carefully place the dumplings on top of the vegetables and sauce and bake for 20 minutes until risen and golden brown. Serve immediately.

Clare's winter-vegetable cobbler

Artichoke and Gorgonzola Pizza

This pizza is ready in next to no time and because of the choice of toppings it looks really quite sophisticated. I always keep a packet of pizza-base mix in the cupboard and there's often a wedge of blue cheese lurking in the back of my fridge, so I find it ideal for entertaining last-minute guests. I often serve my Roast Eggplant and Mint Salad (page 120) or my Fennel, Orange and Olive Salad (page 132) on the side.

PREPARATION: 15 minutes + 10 minutes rising time   COOKING TIME: 20 minutes

SERVES 4

2 x 145 g packages pizza dough mix

250 ml (1 cup) warm water

285 g jar artichokes in olive oil, well drained

150 g (5 oz) Gorgonzola or dolcelatte

freshly ground black pepper

2 tablespoons snipped fresh chives, to garnish

METHOD

1 Pre-heat the oven to 220°C/425°F/Gas 7. Place two large baking sheets in the oven.

2 Empty the pizza dough mix into a large bowl, pour in the warm water, then bring together to make a soft dough. On a floured board, knead the dough vigorously for 5 minutes until smooth and stretchy.

3 Halve the dough and roll each piece into a 23 cm (9 inch) round. Place each circle on to a sheet of floured baking parchment. Arrange the artichokes evenly over each base, then crumble over the cheese; season with black pepper. Leave to rise for 10 minutes.

4 Remove the hot baking sheets from the oven and carefully slide a pizza on to each. Bake for 15–20 minutes until the base is golden and cooked through. Sprinkle with the chives and serve warm.

Caramelized-onion and red-pepper penne

A simple dish that's full of flavor and color, and is so satisfying.

PREPARATION: 10 minutes COOKING TIME: 45 minutes

SERVES 4

4 tablespoons olive oil

4 red peppers, seeded and cut lengthwise into 1 cm wide strips

1 large onion, sliced

300 g (11 oz) dried penne or other pasta shapes

handful of fresh basil

salt and freshly ground black pepper

freshly grated Parmesan, to serve

METHOD

1 Heat the oil in a large, non-stick frying-pan and cook the peppers over a medium heat for 15 minutes. Add the onion and cook for a further 30 minutes until the peppers and onions are very soft and nicely browned. You will need to keep them on a fairly high heat so that the moisture from the vegetables evaporates. Stir from time to time so they don't catch on the bottom and burn and add a splash more oil if they start to stick. Add salt and pepper to taste.

2 Meanwhile, cook the pasta in a large pan of boiling water according to package instructions. Drain the pasta well and return to the pan. Add the pepper mixture and the basil and mix well together.

3 Divide between 4 bowls and sprinkle with freshly grated Parmesan.

CHEF'S TIP: If you have any left-overs, transfer to a heatproof dish, top with a few cubes of mozzarella or grated Cheddar and bake at 200°C/400°F/Gas 6 for 15 minutes or so until piping hot.

Baked hedgehog tatties

My kids go mad for these Baked Hedgehog Tatties. They love the different colors of the herbs, tomatoes, zucchini and mozzarella and adore the taste. Wicked, Dad, wicked!

PREPARATION: 20 minutes COOKING TIME: 1 hour 25 minutes

SERVES 4

4 x 250 g (9 oz) baking potatoes

3 tablespoons olive oil

1 garlic clove, crushed

1 teaspoon chopped fresh rosemary

4 plum tomatoes, thinly sliced lengthwise

4 baby zucchinis, thinly sliced lengthwise

150 g (¾ cup) ball mozzarella, thinly sliced

salt and freshly ground black pepper

METHOD

1 Pre-heat the oven to 200°C/400°F/Gas 6. Scrub, dry and prick the potatoes with a fork. Place them directly on the oven shelf and cook for 1 hour.

2 Meanwhile, mix together the olive oil, garlic and rosemary and some salt and pepper.

3 With oven mitts, take the potatoes out of the oven. Make deep cuts widthways about 1 cm (½ inch) apart in each potato, taking care not to cut right through. Slot the tomatoes, zucchini and mozzarella into the slices, arranging and alternating them so they all fit evenly into the potatoes. If the potato starts to break up, don't worry, just thread a skewer through to keep everything together.

4 Transfer the hot potatoes to a baking sheet and drizzle with the rosemary oil. Bake for a further 20–25 minutes until the cheese is melted and bubbling and the vegetables are tinged with golden brown. Maddie, Jimmy, dinner's ready. Come and get it!

Baked hedgehog tatties

Goats' cheese and beet leaf tortilla

I love the combination of tangy goats' cheese and the slightly bitter beet leaves. You can get beet leaves from your local grocer or look out for salad bags of them in the supermarket. Good alternatives include red chard and spinach. I like to serve this with my Cracked Tapas Patatas Bravas (page 124) or a simple salad.

PREPARATION: 15 minutes COOKING TIME: 10 minutes

SERVES 2

200 g (7 oz) young beet or spinach leaves

2 tablespoons olive oil

1 shallot, thinly sliced

1 garlic clove, thinly sliced

1 teaspoon chopped fresh rosemary

6 eggs

100 g (½ cup) firm, creamy goats' cheese

salt and freshly ground black pepper

METHOD

1 Bring a large pan of salted water to the boil and cook the beet leaves for just 30 seconds. Drain well and cool under cold water.

2 Heat 1 tablespoon of the oil in a 20 cm (8 inch) non-stick frying-pan and cook the shallot and garlic for 3–4 minutes until softened. Add the rosemary and cook for a further 30 seconds.

3 Meanwhile, in a large bowl, whisk together the eggs with some salt and pepper. Then stir through the cooled beet leaves and the onion mixture. Add the remaining oil to the hot pan, pour in the egg mixture and cook for 1 minute or so, stirring until the egg begins to set.

4 Crumble the goats' cheese over the top of the tortilla and continue to cook over a low heat for a further 5 minutes until the egg is almost completely set – take care not to burn the underneath.

5 Pre-heat the grill to medium. Place the pan under the grill for 2–3 minutes until golden brown and completely set. Slice and serve.

Mouth-watering mushroom and salad-onion risotto

Spend a little time next to your cooker for a truly creamy, cheesy, mouth-watering experience. Go on, it's worth it.

PREPARATION: 20 minutes COOKING TIME: 25 minutes

SERVES 4

10 g packet dried porcini mushrooms

300 ml (1 cup) boiling water

25 g (2 tablespoons) butter

1 bunch green onions, thinly sliced

2 garlic cloves, finely chopped

300 g (10 oz) mixed mushrooms, such as chestnut, morel and oyster, sliced

300 g (1½ cups) risotto rice such as Arborio or Carnaroli

600 ml (2 cups) hot vegetable stock

142 ml carton heavy cream

50 g (½ cup) Parmesan, freshly grated

2 tablespoons chopped fresh parsley

salt and freshly ground black pepper

METHOD

1 Place the dried mushrooms in a heatproof bowl and cover with the boiling water. Set aside for 20 minutes.

2 Heat the butter in a large pan and add the green onions, garlic and mushrooms with some salt and pepper and cook gently for 5 minutes until softened. Remove the mixture with a slotted spoon and set aside.

3 Add the rice to the buttery pan and cook for 1 minute. Drain the dried mushrooms, discarding the soaking liquid, chop roughly and add to the pan. Gradually stir in the stock, cooking for about 15 minutes until the grains are almost tender and all the liquid has been absorbed.

4 Stir in the reserved mushroom mixture, the cream and Parmesan and cook for a further 5 minutes, until the grains are completely tender, cover and leave to rest for 3–4 minutes. Stir in the parsley, check the seasoning and serve.

CHEF'S TIP: If your risotto is a little dry by the time you're ready to serve, stir in a splash more cream and a little warm water.

Pecorino tart
with tarragon crust

This is a really stunning tart. It has such a delicious flavor, I just serve it with a classic arugula and cherry-tomato salad for an elegant supper. It will also serve eight as a starter.

PREPARATION: 20 minutes COOKING TIME: 35 minutes

SERVES 6

300 g (1½ cups) all-purpose flour

½ teaspoon salt

150 g (¾ cup) chilled butter, diced

2 tablespoons fresh tarragon, roughly chopped

½ teaspoon dried chili flakes

450 ml (¾ pint) heavy cream

2 large eggs plus 2 yolks

100 g (¾ cup) freshly grated pecorino

METHOD

1   Pre-heat the oven to 200°C/400°F/Gas 6. Place the flour, salt, butter, tarragon and chili flakes in a food processor and whizz until the mixture forms fine crumbs. Pour in 3 tablespoons of very cold water and pulse again to form a firm dough. You may need a little more or less water.

2   Roll the pastry out on a floured surface and use to line a 23 cm (9 inch) loose-bottomed tart tin. Rest the pastry case for 5 minutes, if possible. Prick the base, fill with crumpled foil and bake for 10 minutes then remove the foil. Lower the oven to 180°C/350°F/Gas 4.

3   Beat together the cream and eggs until well blended. Stir in the pecorino and pour into the tart case. Bake for 25 minutes until just set.

4   Carefully remove the tart from the tin and cut into slices. Serve, while still warm, with an arugula and tomato salad.

CHEF'S TIP: Parmesan makes a good substitute for pecorino. Any left-overs are delicious served cold.

If you have time, chill the pastry case in the freezer for 5 minutes before baking the empty pastry case. It sets and rests the pastry and helps prevent shrinkage during cooking.

Pecorino tart with tarragon crust

Super-speedy spaghetti bake

Pasta bakes can take an age to make – not so this one. I use quick-cook pasta and because the pasta's hot when it goes into the oven, it only takes 15 minutes to develop a crispy golden top.

PREPARATION: 10 minutes COOKING TIME: 15 minutes

SERVES 2

225 g (8 oz) dried, quick-cook spaghetti

250 g carton mascarpone

1 teaspoon Dijon mustard

175 g (6 oz) old Cheddar, grated

6 sun-dried tomatoes, finely chopped

2 tablespoons snipped fresh chives

salt and freshly ground black pepper

METHOD

1 Pre-heat the oven to 220°C/425°F/Gas 7. Cook the spaghetti in a large pan of boiling salted water according to package instructions. Drain well and return to the pan. Add the mascarpone and Dijon mustard, stirring until the mascarpone melts around the pasta.

2 Stir in the Cheddar, sun-dried tomatoes and chives and season. Turn into an ovenproof dish and bake for 15 minutes until bubbling and golden brown.

Super-speedy spaghetti bake

Mama's Greek
butter-bean salad

This is a lovely Greek-style salad that my favorite Greek mom, Mama Tahsia, makes. It's substantial enough to serve as a main course with warm pita and a nice glass of chilled white wine.

PREPARATION: 15 minutes

SERVES 4

4 ripe plum tomatoes

2 tablespoons chopped fresh mint

1 small garlic clove, roughly chopped

juice of 1 small lemon

3 tablespoons olive oil

2 x 420 g cans butter beans, drained

75 g (3 oz) pitted black olives

1 small red onion, thinly sliced

200 g (7 oz) feta, roughly cubed

salt and freshly ground black pepper

warm pita, to serve

METHOD

1 Roughly chop one of the tomatoes and place in a blender or mini food processor with half the mint and the garlic and whizz until smooth. Add the lemon juice and olive oil and some salt and pepper and whizz again to make a smooth dressing.

2 Cut the remaining tomatoes into wedges and toss with the butter beans, olives, red onion, feta and dressing. Transfer to serving plates, scatter over the reserved mint and serve with warm pita bread.

CHEF'S TIP: This dish is great served outdoors or as part of a barbecue. For crispy pita, warm them over a barbecue then split in half. Brush the split sides with a little herb oil (mix oil with chopped herbs and seasoning) and return to the barbecue, cut side down, for 2–3 minutes – but not too close to the hot coals – until crisp and golden.

Mama's Greek butter-bean salad

Sweet-potato and coriander mash

This makes a lovely change from everyday mash and can be served in exactly the same way. I like to throw the coriander into the pan of boiling sweet potatoes for just a few seconds before I drain them. It somehow softens the flavor a little while fixing the color at a lovely bright green.

PREPARATION: 5 minutes COOKING TIME: 20 minutes

SERVES 4

1 kg (2¼ lb) sweet potatoes

1 garlic clove, roughly chopped

15 g package of fresh coriander, roughly chopped

3–4 tablespoons crème fraîche or sour cream

salt and freshly ground black pepper

METHOD

1 Bring a large pan of slightly salted water to a boil. Peel and cube the potatoes and add to the pan with the garlic. Return to the boil then simmer for 15–20 minutes until tender. Add the coriander and cook for 10 seconds; drain well, then return to the pan.

2 Set the pan over a gentle flame and stir with a wooden spoon for 1–2 minutes to evaporate any excess water, but be careful not to let the potatoes catch and burn on the bottom of the pan. Turn off the heat and mash well. Add the crème fraîche and some salt and pepper and mash together until smooth and creamy. Serve warm.

CHEF'S TIP: There are two types of sweet potato: the orange-fleshed and the white-fleshed variety. There's little difference in the flavor, but the orange flesh makes such a pretty mash, it's always worth trying to get it if you can. When you're choosing yours, a little scratch on the skin should reveal the colour of the flesh beneath.

Steamed spinach and pickled ginger salad

Japan is the inspiration behind this very simple, tasty salad. It's a lovely accompaniment for fried or oily dishes as it's so clean and fresh tasting.

PREPARATION: 10 minutes + chilling time

SERVES 4

350 g (12 oz) leaf spinach

1 tablespoon pickled ginger

2 tablespoons soy sauce

1 tablespoon sesame seeds

METHOD

1 Wash the spinach well, then cram into a large pan, cover with a tight-fitting lid and cook for 5 minutes, stirring occasionally until evenly wilted. Alternatively, if you've bought your spinach from the supermarket, you can often cook it in the microwave according to the package instructions.

2 Meanwhile, roughly chop the pickled ginger. Drain the spinach well and, while warm, stir through the pickled ginger and soy sauce. Allow to cool completely, then chill for at least an hour or so.

3 Toast the sesame seeds in a frying-pan until golden brown then remove from the heat. To serve, heap the spinach into towers and sprinkle with the toasted sesame seeds.

Soft, bellissima
Dolcelatte polenta

Many people have been put off polenta because, when they've tried it, it was bland and rubbery. Like most grains, polenta is naturally quite plain tasting but this makes it ideal for adding flavorings such as cheese or sun-dried tomatoes, or for serving it as an accompaniment to strong-tasting dishes. In this instance I serve it straight from the pan before it's had a chance to set, but take note, it does set in just a few minutes, so make sure your guests are seated before you dish it up. I like to serve it with roast vegetables such as the roast tomatoes and arugula I pair with my Herbed Couscous Wedges (page 98) and it's absolutely delicious with my One-pot Chunky Beef Bourguignonne (page 82). Most polenta has been treated to make it quick to cook, so make sure you buy a package with the words 'instant' or 'quick cook' on it. If you'd like to see a picture of the finished dish, turn to page 83.

PREPARATION: 10 minutes COOKING TIME: 5 minutes

SERVES 4

½ teaspoon salt

250 g (1¼ cups) instant polenta

200 g (7 oz) dolcelatte, diced

handful of shredded fresh basil

METHOD

1 Bring 1 litre (4 cups) water to a boil in a large pan with the salt. Pour the polenta into the boiling water in a steady stream, stirring continuously. Bubble for a minute or two until smooth and thick.

2 Stir the dolcelatte and shredded basil into the polenta and check the seasoning. Divide between plates and serve immediately.

CHEF'S TIP: To set polenta, omit the cheese and pour the soft polenta on to an oiled baking sheet. Spread out to a thickness of about 1–2 cm (½–¾ inch) and allow to set. Cut the polenta into triangles, fingers or squares then, to serve, shallow-fry until crisp and lightly browned or brush with a little olive oil and crispen under a medium grill – make sure the polenta is warmed through, as it is a cold center that makes it seem rubbery. Sprinkle the cheese on top to serve.

Fiery chickpea
and yogurt salad

Fiery chilies and cooling yogurt contrast beautifully with each other in this simple salad.

PREPARATION: 5 minutes COOKING TIME: 10 minutes

SERVES 4

1 tablespoon olive oil

1 small onion, finely chopped

1 red chili, seeded and finely chopped

1 teaspoon cumin seeds

4 cups chickpeas, drained

1 cup carton Greek-style yogurt

2 tablespoons chopped fresh coriander

salt and freshly ground black pepper

1 lime, cut into wedges, to serve

METHOD

1 Heat the oil in a small frying-pan and cook the onion for 5 minutes until softened and golden. Stir in the chili and cumin seeds and cook for a further 2 minutes. Transfer to a large bowl.

2 Rinse the chickpeas well and stir into the onion mixture. Add the yogurt and coriander and stir well together until the chickpeas are evenly coated. Add salt and pepper to taste. Chill until ready to serve with the lime wedges.

Roast eggplant
and mint salad

Some people would have you believe that you have to salt eggplants before cooking them in order to remove the bitterness. I really don't think it's necessary unless, of course, they're old and leathery. Besides, most eggplant we buy today don't have those bitter juices anyway. Just carefully remove the prickly green stem, slice and use. But, beware, they drink oil like it's going out of fashion, so go easy. This recipe shows you how a little goes a long way. Enjoy!

PREPARATION: 10 minutes COOKING TIME: 30 minutes

SERVES 4

2 large eggplant

2 garlic cloves, quartered

3 tablespoons olive oil

1 shallot, finely chopped

2 tablespoons chopped fresh mint

2 tablespoons chopped fresh coriander

juice of 1 lime

salt and freshly ground black pepper

METHOD

1 Pre-heat the oven to 200°C/400°F/Gas 6. Cube the eggplants and place in a large roasting pan with the garlic and 2 tablespoons of the olive oil. Season with salt and pepper and roast for 25–30 minutes, stirring frequently until golden brown.

2 Remove from the oven and stir in the shallot, mint, coriander, lime juice and remaining olive oil. Season to taste and serve warm or at room temperature.

Roast eggplant and mint salad *with* Spice-roasted butternut squash (page 129)

Rösti dauphinoise

This is a lovely accompaniment for plain roast meats such as a leg of lamb. It is really easy to make and, as the potatoes are grated and not sliced, they cook more quickly than in the original French gratin dauphinoise. Turn to page 77 to see a picture of this dish.

PREPARATION: 20 minutes COOKING TIME: 40 minutes

SERVES 4

500 g (1 lb 2 oz) floury potatoes such as Maris Piper or King Edward

2 garlic cloves, crushed

75 g (3 oz) Gruyère

284 ml carton heavy cream

25 g (2 tablespoons) butter

salt and freshly ground black pepper

METHOD

1 Pre-heat the oven to 180°C/350°F/Gas 4. Peel and coarsely grate the potatoes, ideally using the grating blade on a food processor or by hand using a sturdy box grater.

2 Lightly butter a 1.2 litre (2 pint) deep ovenproof dish such as a soufflé dish. Mix together all the ingredients, then tip into the prepared dish.

3 Dot the top with butter and bake for 40 minutes until golden and cooked through.

Peppy's rice and peas

When I was a child growing up, Sundays wouldn't have been the same in the Harriott household without rice and peas. You can use all sorts of beans and peas, but my mom, Peppy, always preferred kidney beans. Dried are best, if you've got time to soak and boil them, but for convenience I've used canned kidney beans in the recipe below.

PREPARATION: 10 minutes COOKING TIME: 20 minutes

SERVES 4

small spoonful of butter

1 small onion, finely chopped

1 garlic clove, finely chopped

250 g (1 cup) long grain rice

½ teaspoon fresh thyme leaves

125 g (½ cup) creamed coconut, grated

450 ml (1½ cups) vegetable stock

400 g can red kidney beans

1 Scotch bonnet chilli

salt and freshly ground black pepper

METHOD

1 Heat the butter in a large pan and cook the onion and garlic for 3–4 minutes over a low to medium heat until softened. Stir in the rice and glaze the grains in the butter for 1 minute.

2 Stir in the thyme, coconut, vegetable stock and beans. Drop in the whole chili and bring to a boil. Reduce the heat and simmer gently, with the lid on, for approximately 15–18 minutes until the grains are tender and the liquid has been absorbed. Carefully remove the whole chili and discard. Rest for 5 minutes before serving, to allow the rice grains to separate.

Cracked tapas patatas bravas

A classic Spanish side dish, this is often found on the menu in tapas bars and always varies in each establishment. It is basically spiced potatoes and often, though not always, includes tomatoes. Patatas bravas are a delicious snack in their own right, but make a tasty accompaniment to simple dishes such as my Pecorino Tart (page 108) or Beet Leaf and Goats' Cheese Tortilla (page 106).

PREPARATION: 15 minutes COOKING TIME: 15 minutes

SERVES 4

750 g (1½ lb) baby new potatoes, unpeeled

4 garlic cloves, unpeeled

1 tablespoon olive oil

1 small onion, thinly sliced

½ teaspoon crushed chili flakes

½ teaspoon paprika

400 g can chopped tomatoes

1 teaspoon dark brown sugar

2 tablespoons chopped fresh parsley

salt and freshly ground black pepper

METHOD

1 Place the baby potatoes in a clean tea towel and hit with a wooden mallet or rolling pin to crack them lightly. Flatten each garlic clove with the mallet or the blade of a heavy knife.

2 Heat the oil in a large sauté pan and cook the onion, potatoes and garlic for 10–12 minutes, stirring until golden. Add the chili flakes, paprika, tomatoes, brown sugar and some salt and pepper.

3 Cover and simmer for 15 minutes until the potatoes are tender. Stir through the parsley and serve warm.

Ceylonese spiced string beans

Spiced beans make a fantastic accompaniment to curry. This recipe comes courtesy of Lisa who is a real curry queen. Of course you don't have to use string beans, any green bean will do. There is a picture of this dish on page 89.

PREPARATION: 10 minutes COOKING TIME: 5 minutes

SERVES 4

300 g (10 oz) string beans

2 tablespoons sunflower oil

1 garlic clove, finely chopped

½ teaspoon cumin seeds

½ teaspoon mustard seeds

¼ teaspoon ground turmeric

¼ teaspoon ground coriander

2 tomatoes, roughly chopped

1 teaspoon grated ginger root

1 teaspoon fine granulated sugar

½ teaspoon salt

juice of ½ lemon

1 tablespoon chopped fresh coriander

METHOD

1 String the beans then diagonally slice them into 4 cm (1½ inch) lengths. Cook in a pan of boiling salted water for exactly 1 minute, then drain.

2 Heat the oil in a large pan and cook the garlic for 1 minute. Add the cumin and mustard seeds and cook for 1 minute, then add the ground spices and cook for a further minute.

3 Stir in the chopped tomatoes and simmer for 1–2 minutes until softened and a little pulpy. Stir in the beans, ginger, sugar, salt and lemon and simmer together for 3–4 minutes until the beans are tender. Stir in the fresh coriander and serve.

Couscous
with fava beans and bacon

Couscous is now readily available and it's so quick to prepare. By adding fava beans and bacon you have a lovely side dish to accompany almost any main course.

PREPARATION: 15 minutes COOKING TIME: 15 minutes

SERVES 4

1 tablespoon olive oil

1 shallot, finely chopped

1 garlic clove, finely chopped

25 g (2 tablespoons) butter

6 slices bacon, roughly chopped

150 g (5 oz) fava beans, shelled

1 cup couscous

400 ml (2 cups) hot vegetable stock

juice of ½ lemon

2 tablespoons chopped fresh coriander

salt and freshly ground black pepper

METHOD

1 Heat the oil in a large pan and cook the shallot, garlic and bacon for 3–4 minutes until golden. Add the butter, allow to melt, then stir in the beans and couscous and cook for 1 minute, stirring until the couscous is coated in the butter.

2 Pour in the stock, bring to a boil then remove from the heat, cover and allow to cool for 10 minutes until the grains swell and absorb all the liquid.

3 Loosen the grains with a fork and stir through the lemon juice and coriander. Check the seasoning and serve warm or chilled.

Easy pilau rice

Now, for all of you who have problems with cooking pilau rice, this recipe is really very easy and goes exceptionally well with a good curry, like my Madras Coconut, Chicken and Banana Curry on page 69. Have a go, you won't be disappointed. Turn to page 89 to see what the finished dish looks like.

PREPARATION: 20 minutes COOKING TIME: 25 minutes

SERVES 6

4 tablespoons vegetable oil

3 onions, thinly sliced

1 cinnamon stick

1 teaspoon cumin seeds

3 cardamom pods, cracked

3 star anise

500 g (1 lb 2 oz) basmati rice, rinsed

2 teaspoons salt

handful of fresh coriander leaves

METHOD

1 Heat the oil in a large pan and cook half the onions over a fairly high heat for about 10 minutes until crisp and lightly browned. Drain on kitchen paper and set aside, leaving just a coating of oil still in the pan.

2 Add the remaining onions to the pan with the cinnamon, cumin, cardamom and star anise and cook gently for 5 minutes or so until the onions are golden.

3 Add the rice, cook for 1 minute then add 1 litre (4 cups) of water and the salt. Bring to a boil, cover and cook over a low heat for 12 minutes until the grains are tender and the water has been absorbed.

4 Remove from the heat and leave to stand, covered, for 5 minutes, then transfer to a serving dish and sprinkle with the fried onions and coriander leaves; serve warm.

Spice-roasted
butternut squash

Butternut squash is a delicious nutty-tasting vegetable. Roasting brings out its natural sweetness, which is nicely balanced with the spices. This dish is great with grilled fish or meat, or wonderful on its own with a spoonful of plain yogurt. There's a picture of this recipe on page 121 if you want to see what it will look like.

PREPARATION: 10 minutes COOKING TIME: 35 minutes

SERVES 4

1 butternut squash, about 850 g (1 lb 14 oz)

2 tablespoons olive oil

1 teaspoon cumin seeds

1 teaspoon crushed chili flakes

1 teaspoon ground coriander

½ teaspoon sea salt

METHOD

1 Pre-heat the oven to 200°C/400°F/Gas 6. Peel the butternut squash, then halve it lengthways and scoop out and discard the seeds. Cube the flesh.

2 Put the olive oil in a roasting pan and place in the oven.

3 Place the cumin, chili, coriander and salt in a pestle and mortar and crush together lightly. Throw the spices into the hot oil, then add the butternut squash, tossing to coat the pieces in the spiced oil.

4 Roast for 30–35 minutes, turning from time to time until tender and golden brown.

CHEF'S TIP: Try serving this with a spoonful or two of natural yogurt and a dusting of cayenne.

Andalucian garlic bread

Have you got the Andalucian crunch bug? You will after tucking into this. Perfect for a pre-dinner nibble or casual snack.

PREPARATION: 10 minutes + resting time COOKING TIME: 5 minutes

SERVES 4

250 g (9 oz) ripe pomodorino or cherry tomatoes

12 black olives, roughly chopped

1 teaspoon capers, chopped

2–3 tablespoons olive oil

1 tablespoon roughly chopped fresh parsley

1 loaf flat bread such as ciabatta

1 large, juicy garlic clove

salt and freshly ground black pepper

METHOD

1 Place the tomatoes in a large bowl and with your thumb forcefully flatten each tomato so the flesh squashes and the seeds spill out. Mix in the olives, capers, 1 tablespoon of the olive oil, the parsley and some salt and pepper. Set aside at room temperature for at least 30 minutes.

2 Halve the bread horizontally and cut each half into 4 even-sized pieces. Pre-heat a griddle or heavy, non-stick frying-pan. Brush the cut surface of the bread with a little oil and cook in the hot pan for 3–4 minutes until golden brown and a little charred.

3 Cut the garlic clove in half and rub the cut surface over the toasted side of the hot bread. Pile on to a serving platter and casually spoon over the tomato mixture. Serve while still slightly warm.

Andalucian garlic bread

Fennel, orange and olive salad

This very simple, low-fat, Italian peasant-style salad is a lovely, refreshing accompaniment to plain meat and fish dishes. There's a picture of the finished dish on page 57.

PREPARATION: 10 minutes

SERVES 4

1 fennel bulb

1 large orange

12 black olives

1 tablespoon olive oil

1 tablespoon finely chopped red onion

salt and freshly ground black pepper

METHOD

1 Thinly slice the fennel, reserving the frondy herbs from the top. Arrange the slices on a plate.

2 Slice the bottom of the orange so it will sit firmly on the board, then with a small, sharp knife slice off the rind and pith. Slice off any remaining pith at the top of the orange, then cut into thin slices. Arrange the orange slices on the plate with the fennel.

3 Scatter over the olives, olive oil, red onion and the reserved fennel fronds. Season with salt and pepper and serve.

Simple wok noodles

This is a fantastically versatile recipe. When I serve it as a side dish, I leave it plain and simple, but it can easily be turned into a tasty supper with the addition of a little meat or some more vegetables – I sometimes throw in some left-over cooked chicken or pork or a handful of cooked, peeled shrimp. Turn to page 71 to see a picture of the finished dish.

PREPARATION: 10 minutes COOKING TIME: 10 minutes

SERVES 4

250 g (9 oz) Chinese egg noodles

1 tablespoon sunflower oil

150 g (5 oz) shiitake mushrooms, thinly sliced

4 green onions, thinly sliced

1 teaspoon dark soy sauce, plus extra to serve

200 g (1 cup) bean sprouts

sea salt

1 teaspoon sesame oil

METHOD

1 Cook the noodles in a large pan of boiling water, according to the package instructions.

2 Heat the sunflower oil in a wok and when good and hot, stir-fry the mushrooms for 2 minutes. Add the green onions and cook for a further 1 minute. Add the soy sauce.

3 Drain the noodles thoroughly and add to the wok with the bean sprouts, a little salt and the sesame oil. Cook for 2–3 minutes, stirring continuously, until piping hot and well mixed, but don't over cook the bean sprouts – they should still be crunchy. Serve immediately with some extra soy sauce for splashing over.

Velvet vanilla sweet-cream risotto

Okay, so it's a rice pudding, but so delicious! The round, plump risotto grain makes for a lovely texture and the flavor of real vanilla is pretty hard to beat.

PREPARATION: 10 minutes COOKING TIME: 2 hours

SERVES 4

600 ml (2 cups) milk

450 ml (1½ cups) heavy cream

75 g (⅓ cup) light brown sugar

1 vanilla bean

100 g (½ cup) risotto rice such as Arborio or Carnaroli

small spoonful of butter

METHOD

1 Pre-heat the oven to 150°C/300°F/Gas 2. Place the milk, cream and sugar in a pan. Split the vanilla bean and scrape the seeds into the pan, add the pod, then bring to the boil. Remove from the heat.

2 Meanwhile, place the rice in a 1.75 litre (6 cup) pie dish. Remove and discard the bean then pour the hot cream mixture over the rice. Dot the top with butter and bake for 1½–2 hours, stirring occasionally, until thick and creamy. Serve warm or chilled. A little extra drizzling of chilled pouring cream is really nice.

Srikhand
with iced mango shards

When I made this on *Friends for Dinner*, hundreds of people wrote in asking for the recipe. So, here it is, with the addition of some Iced Mango Shards. It's the perfect dessert to serve after a spicy meal, although my family likes to eat it any time.

PREPARATION: 15 minutes, plus chilling time

SERVES 4

¼ teaspoon saffron

2 tablespoons rosewater

1 large mango

1 teaspoon cardamom pods

600 ml (2 cups) Greek-style natural yogurt

25 g (1½ tablespoons) blanched shelled almonds, roughly chopped

50 g (¼ cup) shelled pistachios, roughly chopped

40 g (1 tablespoon) icing sugar

METHOD

1   Mix together the rosewater and saffron and set aside.

2   Slice the mango down either side of the central flat stone then scoop the two halves out of their shells. Thinly slice lengthwise. Arrange on a sheet of wax paper, cover with a second sheet and place in the freezer for at least 1 hour.

3   Place the cardamom pods in a pestle and mortar and lightly crush. Remove and discard the husks, then grind the seeds to a rough powder. Stir the powder into the yogurt with three-quarters of the chopped nuts and the icing sugar. Stir in the rosewater mixture.

4   Divide between 4 glasses then chill for at least an hour. Decorate with the reserved chopped nuts and the sliced, iced mango, to serve.

Cranberry and pomegranate jellies

In my day, 'jelly and evap' was what childhood dreams were made of and I can bet that you really have forgotten just how great they taste together. This jelly is made using cranberry juice, which you can make set very easily using leaf gelatine, and will appeal to adults just as much as kids.

PREPARATION: 10 minutes + setting time

SERVES 4

4 leaves gelatin or 1 x 11.5 g sachet powdered gelatin

600 ml (2 cups) cranberry juice

¼ cup (2 oz) fine granulated sugar

seeds of 1 pomegranate

170 g can evaporated milk

METHOD

1 If using leaf gelatin, place in a bowl and just cover with cold water.

2 Pour the cranberry juice into a pan and stir in the sugar. Heat the juice, but just before it comes to the boil remove from the heat. Allow to cool for 2 minutes.

3 Lift the leaf gelatin out of the water, squeezing to remove the excess liquid. Add to the hot cranberry mixture and stir to dissolve – if using powdered gelatine, dissolve in a little of the warm cranberry juice then stir into the pan. Pour into 4 glasses, then sprinkle in the pomegranate seeds and any juice. They tend to float, making a layer at the top of each glass.

4 Allow the jellies to cool, then chill for at least an hour or until ready to serve. If you like, rest the glasses at an angle in the racked fridge shelf so they set at a slant.

5 Pour the evaporated milk into a jug and allow your guests to mix it into their jelly at the table.

CHEF'S TIP: For an even more adult-friendly jelly, try stirring in a splash of vodka or orange liqueur such as Cointreau or Grand Marnier.

Cranberry and pomegranate jellies

Blue-mountain coffee rum-poached pears

I like to make these with Jamaican Blue-mountain Coffee, but your favorite filter coffee would do nicely.

PREPARATION: 10 minutes + chilling time COOKING TIME: 20 minutes

SERVES 4

300 ml (1 cup) filter or cafetière coffee

40 g (¼ cup) dark brown sugar

1 cinnamon stick

4 dessert pears, such as Rocha or Comice

4 tablespoons dark rum

METHOD

1 Place the coffee in a pan large enough to hold the pears snugly with the sugar and cinnamon and heat gently. Carefully peel the pears, leaving the stalks intact. Poach in the sweetened coffee for 20 minutes, turning occasionally.

2 Turn off the heat, stir in the rum and allow the pears to cool in the coffee mixture. Transfer to a bowl and chill until ready to serve.

3 To serve, place the pear in a pretty, shallow glass dish or bowl and spoon over the coffee syrup.

Ricotta pancakes
with mulled strawberries

Hot fluffy pancakes are something we normally associate with an American holiday. Well here's a recipe that you can make at home, looks gorgeous and tastes sublime.

PREPARATION: 20 minutes COOKING TIME: 20 minutes

SERVES 4

250 g container ricotta

175 ml (¾ cup) milk

4 eggs, separated

100 g (½ cup) all-purpose flour

1 teaspoon baking powder

¼ teaspoon salt

light olive oil, for frying

FOR THE MULLED STRAWBERRIES

225 g (8 oz) small fresh strawberries

150 ml (⅔ cup) fresh orange juice

2 tablespoons fine granulated sugar

1 star anise

1 teaspoon caraway seeds

METHOD

1 Begin with the mulled strawberries. Hull the strawberries, place them in a bowl and set aside.

2 Place the orange juice, sugar, star anise and caraway seeds in a small pan. Bring to the boil and simmer for 5 minutes, then pour over the strawberries and allow to cool. Chill for least an hour and up to 8 hours.

3 Place the ricotta, milk and egg yolks in a large bowl and beat well together to combine. Sift over the flour, baking powder and salt and stir to make a smooth batter.

4 Using an electric whisk, beat the egg whites until stiff. Carefully fold into the batter.

5 Heat a little of the oil in a large, non-stick frying-pan and drop heaped tablespoons of the mixture into the pan. Cook in batches for 1 minute on each side until puffed and golden. Repeat to make 12 pancakes. Divide between 4 plates and spoon over the mulled strawberries.

Six-minute soft-centred chocolate puddings

These are the most fantastic dinner-party desserts. Get the puddings ready and into their tins, then chill. Take them out of the fridge as soon as your guests arrive, so that they return to room temperature, and, as you clear the table after the main course, just slip them into the oven for a truly fabulous chocolate treat.

PREPARATION: 15 minutes COOKING TIME: 6 minutes

SERVES 6

185 g (6½ oz) semi-sweet chocolate

185 g (¾ cup) butter, plus extra for greasing

3 eggs, plus 3 extra yolks

6 tablespoons fine granulated sugar

3 teaspoons all-purpose flour

cocoa powder, for dusting

crème fraîche, to serve

METHOD

1 Pre-heat the oven to 230°C/450°F/Gas 8. Break the chocolate into a heatproof bowl set over a pan of simmering water. Add the butter and leave to melt.

2 In a separate bowl, whisk the eggs, yolks and sugar until thickened. Whisk in the melted chocolate mixture, then sieve over the flour and quickly fold in.

3 Divide the mixture between six buttered moulds or ramekins. Bake the puddings for 6 minutes until the outside is set but the center is still soft.

4 Turn each pudding on to a plate, then gently lift off the moulds. Place a spoonful of crème fraîche on top of each pudding and dust with cocoa. Serve immediately.

CHEF'S TIP: Why not make some hazelnut meringues with the leftover egg whites? Simply beat the whites until stiff, add 75 g (⅓ cup) fine granulated sugar and beat the mixture until glossy. Add 50 g (¼ cup) light-brown sugar and beat again for 1 minute, then fold in 50 g (¼ cup) ground hazelnuts. Spoon onto a lightly oiled baking sheet and bake in a cool oven (110°C/225°F/Gas ½) for just over an hour until they are crisp. When cool, sandwich together with cream and chopped Maltesers.

Six-minute soft-centered chocolate puddings

Oaty gingered plum crumble

There's nothing more satisfying than a delicious oaty crumble with steaming hot custard. So … here it is.

PREPARATION: 15 minutes COOKING TIME: 40 minutes

SERVES 6

750 g (1½ lb) small red plums

2 pieces of stem ginger, finely chopped

50 g (¼ cup) light brown sugar

FOR THE CRUMBLE TOPPING

150 g (¾ cup) all-purpose flour

100 g (½ cup) chilled, diced butter

75 g (⅓ cup) light brown sugar

25 g (2 tablespoons) rolled oats

ice cream, custard or cream, to serve

METHOD

1 Pre-heat the oven to 200°C/400°F/Gas 6. Place the plums in a 1.2 litre (4 cup) ovenproof dish and sprinkle with the ginger and sugar.

2 Rub the butter into the flour until it resembles unevenly sized breadcrumbs. Stir through the sugar and oats and scatter loosely over the fruit, but don't be tempted to pack it down, we want it rough and crumbly.

3 Bake for 35–40 minutes until the plums are soft and the crumble is golden brown. Serve warm with ice cream or custard, or cold with cream.

Turkish-style apricots
with pistachio praline

My sister-in-law, Fatima, used to do a version of these delightful apricots.
I've added my own little twist and come up with a dessert that my wife says is
"to die for."

PREPARATION: 30 minutes + 2 hours chilling time COOKING TIME: 10 minutes

SERVES 6

250 g (9 oz) ready-to-eat dried apricots

50 g (¼ cup) fine granulated sugar

4 cracked cardamom pods

1 teaspoon cracked black peppercorns

juice of ½ lemon

1 cup crème fraîche

FOR THE PRALINE

75 g (⅓ cup) granulated sugar

1 teaspoon sunflower oil

50 g (⅓ cup) pistachio nuts

METHOD

1 Place the apricots in a large pan with 450 ml (1¾ cups) water, the sugar,
cardamom, pepper and lemon juice. Bring to a boil and simmer for
10 minutes. Remove from the heat, allow to cool, then chill for at least 2 hours.

2 For the praline, place the sugar in a small pan with 1 tablespoon of
water. Heat gently, stirring until the sugar dissolves, then bring to a boil
and simmer rapidly until golden brown.

3 While the sugar is boiling, brush a baking sheet with a little oil and
scatter the pistachios over it in an even layer, keeping them all close
together. As soon as the caramel is golden, allow the bubbles to subside,
then pour it over the nuts and leave to cool and set hard. Then, place the
praline on a board and, with a heavy knife, chop into shards.

4 Divide the apricots between 6 bowls and spoon over a couple of
tablespoons of the cooking liquor. Top each serving with a spoonful of
crème fraîche and decorate with the praline shards.

CHEF'S TIP: The praline can be made up to 2 hours in advance and stored
in an air-tight container. The caramel attracts moisture, so any longer than
that and the praline will become a little sticky.

Original baked
lemon and raisin cheesecake

You can't beat an old-fashioned cheesecake, especially when it's full of juicy raisins and has a fresh lemon zingy taste. I've substituted the heavy cream cheese that you find in traditional cheesecakes for a mixture of mascarpone and crème fraîche, so that it's nice and light.

PREPARATION: 20 minutes + cooling time COOKING TIME: 40 minutes

SERVES 6

150 g (5 oz) graham crackers

50 g (¼ cup) butter, melted

2 cups mascarpone

1 cup crème fraîche

2 egg yolks

100 g (½ cup) fine granulated sugar

2 tablespoons cornstarch

75 g (½ cup) golden raisins

grated rind of 1 lemon

icing sugar, for dusting

cream, to serve

METHOD

1 Pre-heat the oven to 190°C/375°F/Gas 5. Place the graham crackers in a strong plastic bag and crush with a rolling pin to form crumbs. Mix with the melted butter and press into the base of a 20 cm (8 inch) spring-form cake tin. Pop into the freezer for 5 minutes or so to set.

2 Using electric beaters, mix together the mascarpone, crème fraîche, egg yolks, granulated sugar and cornstarch until well blended. Stir in the raisins as and lemon rind and spoon over the crumb base, smoothing over the surface.

3 Place on a baking sheet and bake for 40 minutes until golden – it will still be fairly wobbly, but don't worry, it will set as it cools. The cake sometimes cracks, but you can avoid this by allowing it to cool slowly – turn off the oven, open the door and allow it to cool as the oven does.

4 When completely cool, place in the fridge for at least an hour or two, but preferably overnight. Carefully remove from the tin and dust with icing sugar. Slice into wedges and serve with a drizzle of cream.

Original baked lemon and raisin cheesecake

Lemon and blueberry
surprise pudding

This is one of those lovely desserts where the top of the pudding is a delicious, moist sponge and the bottom separates out into a thick, lemony custard. Two puddings for the price of one! It's equally good eaten the next day, straight out of the fridge, although I don't expect there'll be any left.

PREPARATION: 20 minutes COOKING TIME: 45 minutes

SERVES 6

100 g (½ cup) butter, plus a little extra, for greasing

175 g (⅞ cup) light brown sugar

grated rind and juice of 2 lemons

4 eggs, separated

50 g (¼ cup) all-purpose flour

125 g container fresh blueberries

500 ml (2 cups) milk

METHOD

1 Pre-heat the oven to 180°C/350°F/Gas 4. Lightly butter a 2 litre (8 cup) ovenproof dish. With an electric whisk, beat the butter and sugar until pale and fluffy. Add the lemon juice and rind, followed by the egg yolks, one at a time until well blended – if the mixture looks a little curdled at this stage, don't worry.

2 Sift over the flour and stir in, followed by the blueberries and milk.

3 Rinse off the beaters then whisk the egg whites until they form soft peaks; don't allow them to get too stiff or they will be difficult to fold into the mixture and you will end up losing all the air you've just beaten in.

4 With a large metal spoon gradually fold the egg whites into the blueberry mixture. Pour into the dish, place on a baking sheet and bake for 40–45 minutes until risen, golden and firm to the touch.

Lemon and blueberry surprise pudding

Peppered pineapple tart tatin

A wonderful combination that works so well that when friends come round for dinner they all want a copy of the recipe. Want to know why? Just try it and see for yourself!

PREPARATION: 15 minutes COOKING TIME: 25 minutes

SERVES 6

50 g (¼ cup) butter

75 g (⅓ cup) fine granulated sugar

1 teaspoon cracked black peppercorns

454 g can of mini pineapple rings, halved into semi-circles

375 g ready-rolled shortcrust puff pastry

vanilla or Bailey's ice cream, to serve

METHOD

1 Pre-heat the oven to 200°C/400°F/Gas 6. Heat the butter over a medium high heat in a 24 cm (9½ inch) skillet. Add the sugar and cook for 3–4 minutes, stirring occasionally, until caramel colored.

2 Toss in the peppercorns then, using a fork or tongs to pick them up, gently lay the pineapple rings in the pan – be very careful as the caramel is very hot. Open out the pastry and cut roughly into a 28 cm (11 inch) circle. Place the pastry on top of the pan and roughly tuck in the edges, using a fork. Bake for 25 minutes until the pastry is risen and deep golden.

3 Remove the tart from the oven, leave to rest for 5 minutes, then place a large plate on top. Invert the tart on to the plate, slice and serve with ice cream.

CHEF'S TIP: You could also try using fresh pineapple for this recipe.

Peppered pineapple tart tatin

Gran's baked buttered apples

It's nice to eat something sweet that reminds us of our childhood, and baked apples definitely fall into that category. This recipe is delicious, with lots of fruit and nuts, a touch of spice and a good dollop of vanilla ice cream – ooh, I might just start sucking my thumb again!

PREPARATION: 15 minutes COOKING TIME: 40 minutes

SERVES 4

4 large eating apples

50 g (¼ cup) fresh white breadcrumbs

½ teaspoon ground ginger

25 g (2 tablespoons) light brown unrefined sugar

25 g (2 tablespoons) hazelnuts, chopped

25 g (2 tablespoons) small golden raisins

25 g (2 tablespoons) butter

vanilla ice cream, to serve

METHOD

1 Preheat the oven to 180°C/350°F/Gas 4. Using an apple corer, remove the core from each apple, leaving a cavity roughly 2 cm (¾ inch) across. Butter a small ovenproof dish and sit the apples in the dish.

2 Mix together the breadcrumbs, ginger, sugar, nuts and raisins. Carefully spoon this mixture into the center of the apples. Dot the top with the remaining butter, then bake for 35–40 minutes until the apples are completely tender with split skins.

3 Transfer to serving plates, scraping up any pan sediment. Serve warm with a scoopful of ice cream.

Gran's baked buttered apples

Passion fruit soufflé shells

If you're looking for a dessert that's truly stunning, look no further. These passion fruit shells really do titillate those tastebuds!

PREPARATION: 15 minutes COOKING TIME: 8 minutes

SERVES 4

6 large passion fruit

100 ml (½ cup) milk

1 egg, separated

40 g (¼ cup) light brown sugar

2 teaspoons all-purpose flour

icing sugar, for dusting

METHOD

1 Pre-heat the oven to 200°C/400°F/Gas 6. Halve the passion fruit lengthwise and scoop the flesh and seeds into a small bowl.

2 Cut a small slice off the base of the passion fruit shells and sit them snugly side by side in a heatproof dish.

3 Gently warm the milk, but don't allow it to boil. Meanwhile, using a hand whisk, beat the egg yolk with about half the sugar until pale and light. Whisk in the flour and then the milk, over a low heat, beating until smooth. Cook gently for 2 minutes until thickened, then remove from the heat. Stir in 2 tablespoons of the passion fruit pulp and seeds.

4 Whisk the egg white until it forms soft peaks, then add the remaining sugar and whisk until fairly stiff. Gently fold into the custard then divide between the passion fruit shells. Bake for 8 minutes until risen and golden.

5 Meanwhile, pass the remaining passion fruit pulp and seeds through a sieve into a small bowl. Discard the seeds and reserve the juice. Pour the juice into a small pan and heat gently for 2–3 minutes, stirring until slightly thickened.

6 Place 3 soufflé shells on each of 4 serving plates and drizzle round the passion fruit juice. Dust with icing sugar and serve immediately, as they will start to sink as soon as they come out of the oven.

Passion fruit soufflé shells

Basque custard and almond tart with raspberries

A Spanish sweet-custard tart that's lovely either warm or chilled.

PREPARATION: 20 minutes COOKING TIME: 30 minutes

SERVES 6

300 g (10 oz) ready-made sweet shortcrust pastry

200 g (1 cup) fine granulated sugar

1 tablespoon cornstarch

300 ml (1 cup) milk

4 egg yolks

25 g/1 oz butter, diced

½ teaspoon vanilla extract

125 g (4½ oz) fresh raspberries

50 g (¼ cup) flaked almonds

icing sugar, for dusting

METHOD

1 Pre-heat the oven to 180°C/350°F/Gas 4. Use the pastry to line a shallow 23 cm (9 inch) fluted flan tin. Fill with crumpled foil and bake blind (empty) for 10 minutes until set and golden.

2 Place the sugar and cornstarch in a pan and stir in the milk until well blended. Bring to the boil then remove from the heat. Allow to cool a little, then beat in the egg yolks, butter and vanilla extract.

3 Scatter the raspberries over the base, then carefully pour in the custard and sprinkle with the flaked almonds. Bake for 20 minutes until just set and golden. Dust with a little icing sugar and serve warm or cold – it will set more firmly when cool.

INDEX

Page numbers in **bold** indicate recipes
Page numbers in *italics* refer to illustrations

ACKNOWLEDGEMENTS

It's always a pleasure to work with people who are as enthusiastic about food as you are, and this was certainly the case with *Gourmet Express 2*. So, a very special thank you to Silvana Franco, my friend and often my inspiration. Her dedication was exemplary, her hair funky and her lipstick bright and glossy. Also to the lovely Clare Lewis for her hard work, endless shopping, dish preparation, and that cheeky smile – Andy's a lucky man.

A cookery book linked to a television series can be a winning combination, especially if the programmes are made well. With a team made up of executive producer Nick Vaughan-Barratt, producer Sara Kozak, director Stuart Bateup, assistant producer Melanie Stanley, researcher Ruth Mills, production manager Tracey Bagley, PA Alex Johnston, cameraman Pete Coley, sound recordist Cormac Tohill, lighting gaffer Doug Goddard and stylist Lucyina Moodie, we all knew we were doing something very special and I thank them all.

It's been great to have such a special relationship with BBC Books over the years, none more so than with my commissioning editor Nicky Copeland, who really knows how to bring out the best in me. Thanks to project editor Rachel Copus, for dotting my 'i's, crossing my 't's, and occasionally giving me a metaphorical kick up the backside. Also to designer Susannah Good, and daddy photographers Craig Easton and Gus Filgate – they never let you down; thanks, guys. Thanks to my well-travelled friends and agents Jeremy Hicks and Sarah Dalkin, who have eaten their way through the States. And finally, thanks to my adored family: Clare, my wife, who keeps me smiling, feeling good and knows when to deliver that perfect cuppa tea, our fantastic kids Jimmy-roo and Maddie-moopops too, and Oscar-poska-piddily-poo, the pet dog.